SELECTS

Baseball's

100

Greatest
Players

SECOND EDITION

Written by
Ron Smith

Credits

The author: Ron Smith, a senior editor for Sporting News, has written 18 books, including TSN's *Heroes of the Hall*, *The Ballpark Book*, *61** and *Baseball's 25 Greatest Moments*. Smith, a native of Independence, Mo., lives in St. Louis with his wife Christine.

Contributing editors: Dale Bye, Tom Gatto, Joe Hoppel, Leslie McCarthy, Stan McNeal, Conor Nicholl, Shawn Reid, David Robb and Dave Sloan.

Book design: Chad Painter. **Cover design:** Chad Painter. **Photo editor:** Albert Dickson.

Page design and production: Chad Painter, Bob Parajon, Russ Carr, Kristin Bressert.

Photo research: Jim Meier. **Prepress specialists:** Steve Romer, Vern Kasal, Pamela Speh.

Photo Credits

T—top, B—bottom

Sporting News Archives — Front cover (Ruth), Back cover, 2-3,5, 10, 11(2), 14(2), 15, 16(2), 17, 22, 23(2), 24(2), 25, 28(2), 29, 32(2), 33, 34(2), 35, 36(2), 37, 40(2), 41, 42(2), 43, 46T, 48, 49T, 51, 58(2), 59, 62(2), 63, 65T, 68, 69(2), 72, 73(2), 80, 80-81, 81T, 82(2), 83, 84(2), 85, 86(2), 87, 88T, 89, 94(2), 95, 96, 97(2), 98(2), 99, 100(2), 101, 102, 103(2), 104, 105T, 108T, 109(2), 117, 118, 119(2), 124, 125(2), 130, 131(2), 138, 139(2), 144(2), 145, 150, 151(2), 156(2), 157, 158B, 162(2), 163, 165, 166, 167(2), 168(2), 169, 176(2), 177, 184(2), 185, 186(2), 187, 188, 189(2), 190, 191(2), 194, 195(2), 196(2), 197, 198(2), 199, 213T, 224

Malcolm Emmons — 12, 13(2), 18, 44, 45T, 46B, 53B, 64, 65B, 66, 76T, 77, 78T, 79, 106, 120, 129T, 134, 154, 159, 160, 171, 178, 179(2)

Photo File — 19(2), 26, 27(2), 30(2), 31, 52, 54B, 55, 57, 67(2), 88B, 90(2), 91, 116(2), 123(2), 135B, 140B, 141, 155(2), 170(2), 210B

Albert Dickson/Sporting News — 6-7, 9, 20T, 38, 114, 115B, 126T, 126-127, 132T, 133, 173T, 201, 204B, 213B, 216-217, 217, 218-219

Robert Seale/Sporting News — Front cover (Clemens), 8, 21, 39B, 152T, 183B, 208T

Bob Leverone/Sporting News —173B, 204T, 219

Sean Gallagher/Sporting News — 153

Rich Pilling/Sporting News Archives — 39T, 70(2), 92, 93, 110T, 110B, 111, 115T, 121B, 127T, 172, 174, 175B, 192(2), 193, 202T, 203(2), 206(2), 212, 214(2), 215

Rich Pilling/MLB — 45B, 71, 107(2), 137T, 143B, 161, 181

Louis Requena/MLB — 47, 122, 128, 129B, 136, 137B, 158T, 210T, 211

Tony Tomsic/MLB — 142

Dilip Vishwanat/Sporting News Archives — 205

Ed Nessen/Sporting News Archives — 182, 183T

John Cordes for TSN — 132B, 152B, 216, 218

Bernie Nunez for Sporting News — 208B, 209

Thomas E. Witte for Sporting News — 200(2)

Lewis Portnoy/Spectra-Action Inc. — 74B, 75, 76B, 180B

Otto Greule/Getty Images — 20B

T.G Higgins/Getty Images — 207

Negro League Baseball Museum — 49B, 105B, 148(2), 149

Major League Baseball Archives — 50(2)

Courtesy of Pittsburgh Pirates — 53T

UPI/Corbis Bettmann — 54T, 56B, 135T

Courtesy of Baltimore Orioles — 56T

Copyright Philadelphia Phillies — 74T

Courtesy of Cincinnati Reds — 78B

Al Tielmans/Duomo — 121T

Mitchell Layton/Duomo — 175T

Courtesy of Atlanta National League Baseball Inc. — 140T

Courtesy of Baltimore Orioles — 143T

National Baseball Hall of Fame Library Cooperstown — 146(2), 147

Courtesy of Boston Red Sox — 161T

Courtesy of Pittsburgh Pirates — 180T

ISBN 10: 0-89204-800-X

10 9 8 7 6 5 4 3 2 1

FOREWORD *by*
ROGER CLEMENS

From the time he was a young fan in Houston to his days under noted University of Texas baseball coach Cliff Gustafson to his two decades-plus of superstardom in the major leagues, Roger Clemens has been passionate about the game— and driven to excel.

I've been blessed to be able to play and work at a game I love very much. It is a life experience because, in many ways, it teaches you the game of life.

Growing up in Houston and watching Ryan, Seaver, Gibson and the Big Red Machine come to town ... wow, what fun times as a kid. Later, it was on to the University of Texas. "The University." That's where I learned about winning and tradition. Names that will always be in my mind ... Coach Royal, Earl Campbell, Coach Gus. All winners.

Then, playing for the Red Sox,

and the Yankees, teams and cities also rich in history and tradition. Playing with possible future Hall of Famers. Meeting Hall of Famers at old-timers games and wondering if my path would lead that way. Never dreaming that I would reach out and touch men with 300 wins and 4,000 strikeouts.

Having the chance to challenge my favorite hitter, Reggie Jackson, and talk baseball with guys like Williams, Yogi, Mantle, Koufax and Drysdale. Reading and learning the

> **"It couldn't have worked out any better. I'm very fortunate to be able to do it here, in this stadium, in this uniform. Four thousand and 300 puts me with some great men."**
>
> *After victory No. 300 and strikeout No. 4,000 in a 5-2 victory over the Cardinals in 2003 at Yankee Stadium.*

history of the great ones ... Joe Wood, Christy Mathewson, Walter Johnson and, of course, Denton "Cy" Young.

I tell people that my career hasn't happened by accident. Guys that have worked with me on and off the field know what I'm talking about.

> **"The phone call that I received was as exciting as it was the first time I won it. I was glad I was able to bring some excitement to my hometown of Houston."**
>
> *After winning his seventh Cy Young Award in 2004, his first season with the Astros.*

Having a mother who passed down her will and desire. Showing me that working hard and falling short means having no regrets. Picking yourself up and doing it again and again until you get it right. Knowing that heart and soul are far greater than 95 mph and 400 feet—even though 95 mph down and away is pretty good at times!

I found out what it's like to go full circle in a career. Being able to come back home to Houston and work. Still playing at a high level and competing for a championship. Getting fans fired up and having them release some energy. Sharing with them the Cy Youngs, the MVP, the wins, the strikeouts and the World Series championships.

It's our game, the game I love, and the game I will miss playing one day.

Thanks,
Rocket

Roger Clemens

> " Babe was no ordinary man ... Ruth possessed a magnetism that was positively infectious. When he entered a clubhouse or a room, when he appeared on the field, it was as if he was the whole parade. There seemed to be flags waving, bands playing constantly. "

WAITE HOYT

BABE RUTH

Babe Ruth played baseball like he lived his life: with loud, gaudy, entertaining gusto. There was nothing subtle about the happy-go-lucky Sultan of Swat, who paraded through his career, forged an enduring relationship with adoring fans and then withstood the test of time as the greatest power hitter in baseball history.

Ruth's legendary home run totals—714 in his career, 60 in 1927—are no longer records, but they still stand as milestone numbers by which all power hitters are judged. His legendary carousing still enhances the irascible image that colors his aura. More than anything, the magnetic Ruth is hailed as the savior of the game, the man who ushered in the longball era and revitalized baseball when it was mired in the bog of the 1919 Black Sox scandal.

The Babe, a former Baltimore orphan, actually started his career as a 6-foot-2 lefthanded pitcher who carved out a 94-46 regular-season record and 3-0 World Series mark for the Boston Red Sox from 1914-19. But the real Ruth emerged in 1919 with a major league-record 29 homers and soared to a mind-boggling total of 54 in 1920, his first season as a full-time right fielder with the New York Yankees. The race was on.

Ruth became a New York icon as he powered his way through the Roaring '20s and the Great Depression, posting shocking homer totals of 59 (1921), 60 (1927) and 54 (1928) while leading the Yankees to four World Series championships and anchoring one of the most devastating line-ups in history. Lost in the fog of Ruth's 12 American League home run titles, 13 slugging championships, four 50-homer seasons and six RBI titles was a career .342 average that still ranks 10th all time.

Not lost is the image of a paunchy Babe signing autographs, posing with celebrities, cavorting with kids or circling the bases with his distinctive trot. When he retired in 1935 at age 40 after one season with the Boston Braves, the Bambino owned every slugging record in the game—and enduring recognition as its most colorful and dynamic superstar.

THE ROARING '20s

The immortal Ruth dominated the 1920s (1920-29) like no power hitter since has dominated a decade:

HRs	Player	Decade
467	Babe Ruth	1920s
415	Jimmie Foxx	1930s
405	Mark McGwire	1990s
393	Harmon Killebrew	1960s
326	Duke Snider	1950s
313	Mike Schmidt	1980s
296	Willie Stargell	1970s
234	Ted Williams	1940s

"There'll be another regular Giants center fielder some day, but never another Willie Mays."

BARRY BONDS

THE SPORTING NEWS, 1990

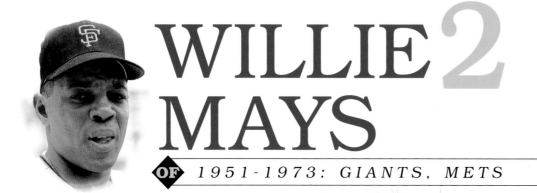

WILLIE 2 MAYS

He might have been as close to baseball perfection as we'll ever get. And from the moment you walked into the stadium and took your seat, through the final out of every game, your eyes, by sheer magnetic force, were drawn to the youthful smile, the boundless enthusiasm and the graceful athleticism of Willie Mays.

The "Say Hey Kid," the former New York and San Francisco Giants star who set the lofty standard by which center fielders will forever be judged, could dominate games in ways beyond comprehension. He was the classic five-tool star with blazing speed and equally fast instincts, powerful arms that could launch balls out of any ballpark and a sculpted 5-foot-11 body that was durable enough to withstand 13 seasons of 150-plus games.

Baseball lore is filled with accounts of incredible Mays catches and throws. He showcased his daring baserunning in a record-tying 24 All-Star Games. He was a career .302 hitter who could break up a pitching duel with an opposite-field bloop single or a 450-foot home run. He was a batting champion, four-time homer leader, two-time MVP and full-time offensive grinder who topped 300 total bases in 13 straight seasons.

Mays made an indelible stamp on the record books with 660 home runs (fourth on the all-time list), 3,283 hits (10th) and top 10 rankings in runs (2,062), RBIs (1,903), total bases (6,066) and other categories. But memories somehow gravitate toward the graceful ease with which he made difficult defensive plays look easy and the instinctive acceleration around second base on balls into the gap.

Mays is personified by the back-to-the-infield catch he made in Game 1 of the 1954 World Series, setting the stage for the Giants' shocking sweep of Cleveland. But he also is remembered for his 1961 four-homer game at Milwaukee and numerous other spectacular moments that defined a 22-year career that stretched from 1951, when he helped the Giants stage the most dramatic pennant run in history, to a 1973 finale with the New York Mets.

THE 600 CHASE

Mays was the fifth player to reach the 500 career home run milestone, and the second to reach the more exclusive 600-homer plateau:

Player	500th	600th
Babe Ruth	1st	1st
Jimmie Foxx	2nd	
Mel Ott	3rd	
Ted Williams	4th	
Willie Mays	5th	2nd
Mickey Mantle	6th	
Eddie Mathews	7th	
Hank Aaron	8th	3rd
Ernie Banks	9th	
Harmon Killebrew	10th	

TY 3 COBB

No player in history generated more emotion, created more havoc, bruised more egos and left more battlescars than Tyrus Raymond Cobb, a snarling wildcat who cut a bloody path to baseball immortality with a take-no-prisoners style, razor-sharp spikes, iron fists and a tongue that spared nobody, friend or foe.

Exactly what motivated the 6-foot-1, 175-pound Georgia Peach remains a dark mystery. But his incredible talents were fueled by equal parts anger, intensity, cunning, intimidation and a mean-spirited, win-at-all-costs drive that never wavered over an incredible 22 seasons with the Detroit Tigers and two with the Philadelphia Athletics. Cobb was a bully and a brawler, but he also was the dominant player of the dead-ball era and his near-legendary feats have withstood the test of time.

Cobb was to bat control what Babe Ruth was later to the home run. A lefthanded hitter, he choked up on the bat with a split grip and drove the ball anywhere he wanted. If muscle was required, Cobb could supply it, and he was a master bunter. But he was most dangerous on the bases, where he used his speed to dominate and his spikes to deliver bloody messages.

Love him or hate him, this was no ordinary demon. When Cobb retired in 1928 at age 42, he owned an incredible 90 all-time records. His 12 American League batting titles (nine in succession) and .366 career average still top the all-time charts. His career records of 897 stolen bases, 2,246 runs scored and 4,191 hits have been broken, but not erased from baseball lore. Cobb, a three-time .400 hitter who helped the Tigers to three straight pennants (1907-09) but never played on a World Series winner, also was an accomplished outfielder with speed and an above-average arm.

Unpopular and feared, Cobb still earned grudging respect from the baseball world with his inspired play. When the first class of Hall of Fame players was elected in 1936, he garnered 98.2 percent of the vote—easily topping the second-place total of 95.1 shared by Babe Ruth and Honus Wagner.

HOW COBB RANKS ALL-TIME

Seasons	24 (T5th)
Games	3,035 (5th)
Average	.366 (1st)
.300 Seasons	23 (1st)
Batting Titles	12 (1st)
At-bats	11,434 (5th)
Runs	2,246 (2nd)
Hits	4,191 (2nd)
200 Hits	9 (2nd)
Singles	3,053 (2nd)
Doubles	724 (4th)
Triples	295 (2nd)
Total Bases	5,854 (4th)
RBIs	1,938 (5th)
Stolen Bases	897 (4th)

> 66 He could do everything better than any player I ever saw. He was always the first one to detect weaknesses or mistakes by the opposition and benefit by the same. 99
>
> WALTER JOHNSON
>
> THE SPORTING NEWS, 1940

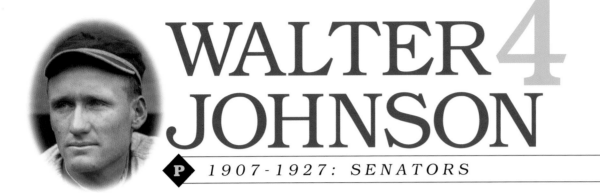

WALTER JOHNSON 4

P *1907-1927: SENATORS*

He was the hardest-throwing pitcher of his era, the most successful fireballer in major league history. Walter Johnson was to power pitching what contemporary Ty Cobb was to bat control. And every time Johnson delivered his fastball to overmatched hitters, he delivered a dose of much-needed pride to the fans of an overmatched franchise.

The 6-foot-1, 200-pound Johnson used that fastball and pinpoint control to carve out 417 victories for the Washington Senators, a career total that ranks second all-time to Cy Young. He slingshotted his heat homeward with a long right arm from an exaggerated sidearm motion, mesmerizing befuddled hitters. For the first 15 years of his 21 major league seasons, that fastball was his only pitch—an incredible testimony to the outstanding 2.17 ERA Johnson compiled over 5,914⅓ innings.

Johnson's success can be measured against two additional barriers that would have been the demise of many pitchers: First, he piled up his wins for the lowly Senators, a team that did not taste success until 1924 and '25—when Johnson was approaching age 40. Second, the "Big Train" never deviated from a gentlemanly demeanor that kept him from brushing back aggressive hitters, allowing them a sense of security they did not enjoy against more mean-spirited pitchers of the era.

Those handicaps never seemed to matter. Fourth-year man Johnson recorded the first of 10 straight 20-win seasons in 1910 and topped the 30 plateau in 1912 and '13—a campaign in which he recorded a 1.14 ERA. From 1910-19, he led the American League nine times in strikeouts, five times in innings and four times in ERA while pitching 78 of his record 110 career shutouts.

Johnson, baseball's first 3,000-strikeout pitcher and, amazingly, a 1-0 loser 26 times, was nearing the end of his career when the Senators finally won their first two pennants. His Game 7 relief win in 1924 gave the city its first championship and he won two games in a losing 1925 Series effort. Johnson was one of five charter members of the Hall of Fame's first class in 1936.

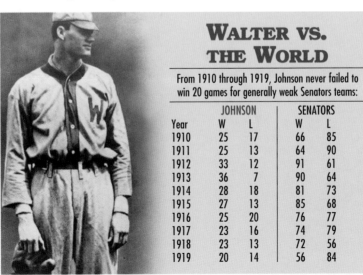

WALTER VS. THE WORLD

From 1910 through 1919, Johnson never failed to win 20 games for generally weak Senators teams:

	JOHNSON		SENATORS	
Year	W	L	W	L
1910	25	17	66	85
1911	25	13	64	90
1912	33	12	91	61
1913	36	7	90	64
1914	28	18	81	73
1915	27	13	85	68
1916	25	20	76	77
1917	23	16	74	79
1918	23	13	72	56
1919	20	14	56	84

HANK AARON 5

He was quiet, unassuming and shy, but no one in the second half century exerted more influence on the record books than Henry Aaron. He mesmerized teammates and fans with a soft-spoken dignity that defined his off-field personality for almost a quarter century while delivering a less-subtle message with the booming bat that helped him find baseball immortality.

That the home run would become Aaron's legacy seemed preposterous when he stepped onto the field as a skinny 6-foot rookie. But no one could have envisioned the unflinching work ethic and competitive fire that would allow Hammerin' Hank to pile up a record 755 home runs over a career that started in 1954 with the Milwaukee Braves and ended 23 seasons later in the same city with the American League's Brewers.

Aaron was a righthanded hitter with a fluid swing and lightning reflexes, but his secret was in the wrists—powerful wrists that allowed him to keep his hands back and drive the ball to all fields with tremendous force. The numbers never were spectacular—eight 40-homer seasons, never more than 47; 11 100-RBI seasons, never more than 132—but the bottom lines were: 3,771 hits (third all-time), 2,174 runs (tied for third), 2,297

RBIs (first), 6,856 total bases (first), a career .305 average with two batting titles and, of course, the homers—41 more than Babe Ruth's previous record.

Lost in the glare of the home run mountain that Aaron finally scaled in a festive 1974 season was his all-around consistency. He had outstanding speed, good instincts and one of the game's better right-field arms—tools that earned him three Gold Gloves. The man who hit 20-plus homers in 20 straight seasons also appeared in a record-tying 24 All-Star Games.

The power combination of Aaron and Eddie Mathews drove the Braves to consecutive Milwaukee pennants and a World Series victory (1957), but the Braves' Atlanta teams generally were weak. One of Aaron's signature moments came late in his MVP 1957 season—an 11th-inning home run that clinched Milwaukee's first pennant.

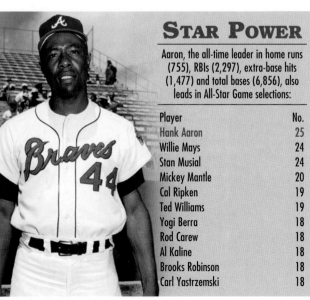

STAR POWER

Aaron, the all-time leader in home runs (755), RBIs (2,297), extra-base hits (1,477) and total bases (6,856), also leads in All-Star Game selections:

Player	No.
Hank Aaron	25
Willie Mays	24
Stan Musial	24
Mickey Mantle	20
Cal Ripken	19
Ted Williams	19
Yogi Berra	18
Rod Carew	18
Al Kaline	18
Brooks Robinson	18
Carl Yastrzemski	18

BARRY 6 BONDS

H is cool, nonchalant, chip-on-the-shoulder attitude can be annoying. So can the arrogance and supreme confidence with which Barry Bonds practices his craft. But there's no denying the San Francisco Giants' handsome left fielder has more than lived up to his swagger while etching his niche among the greatest names in baseball history.

Bonds, like no player before him, has continued to improve with age. He began his career as Pittsburgh's leadoff man, a 6-1, 185-pound basestealing instigator. By 1993, his first season with San Francisco, he had evolved into a solid run-producer. And by 2000, he was a 6-2, 225-pound hitting machine, one of the most feared sluggers ever to play the game. At age 37 in 2001, he set single-season records for home runs (73) and slugging percentage (.863); at age 40 in 2004, he batted an N.L.-leading .362 with 45 homers, 101 RBIs and a mind-boggling 232 walks.

It's all in the genes for Bonds, who, like his father more than two decades ago, brings a superior combination of power, grace, agility and speed to every game. His left-handed swing is fluid, and his strength and hand/eye coordination are borderline legendary. Seven N.L. MVP awards. Eight 40-homer seasons. A 10-time league leader in walks. Twelve 100-RBI seasons. Twelve 100-run campaigns. Two batting titles. Seven slugging championships. Eight Gold Gloves. The numbers are staggering for the best all-around player since Willie Mays.

The Bonds legacy does not end there. In 1998, he became the game's first 400-homer, 400-steal superstar. In 2001, he surged past the 500-homer mark and a year later the 600-homer plateau. In 2004, Bonds became baseball's third 700-homer man. Needing only 11 home runs to catch Babe Ruth and 52 to match Hank Aaron's all-time record, Bonds spent most of 2005 recovering from a knee injury. Limited to 14 games, he hit five homers, setting the stage for an intriguing 2006.

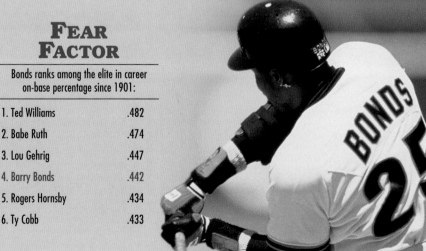

FEAR FACTOR

Bonds ranks among the elite in career on-base percentage since 1901:

1. Ted Williams	.482
2. Babe Ruth	.474
3. Lou Gehrig	.447
4. Barry Bonds	.442
5. Rogers Hornsby	.434
6. Ty Cobb	.433

LOU 7 GEHRIG

1B *1923-1939: YANKEES*

Lou Gehrig will forever be lost in the glare of New York Yankees teammate Babe Ruth's vast spotlight. But nothing about Gehrig's accomplishments should be minimized, from the 2,130 consecutive games he once played as the Iron Horse to his longtime link with Ruth as the enforcer of baseball's original Bash Brothers.

Gehrig was a rock-solid 6-foot, 210-pound left-handed slasher who rocketed line drives to all sections of the park, unlike the towering, majestic home runs that endeared Ruth to adoring fans. And unlike the gregarious Ruth, Gehrig was withdrawn, modest and unassuming, happy to let his teammate drink the fruits of their tandem celebrity. But those who played with and against Gehrig understood the power he could exert over a game.

As the Yankees' first baseman, cleanup hitter and lineup protection for Ruth, Gehrig was an RBI machine. He won four American League titles and tied for another and his 184-RBI explosion in 1931 is a still-standing A.L. record. His 13 consecutive 100-RBI seasons—he averaged an incredible 147 from 1926-38—were a byproduct of 493 career home runs and a not-so-modest .340 average.

It's hard to overstate the havoc wreaked by

Gehrig's bat. He topped 400 total bases in five seasons, topped 150 RBIs seven times, hit a record 23 grand slams, won a 1934 Triple Crown, hit four homers in one 1932 game and cranked out a World Series average of .361 with 10 homers and 34 RBIs. In 1927, when Ruth hit his record 60 home runs, Gehrig quietly batted .373 with 47 homers and 175 RBIs.

The Ruth-Gehrig relationship powered the Yankees to three World Series championships, and when Ruth left New York after the 1934 season, Gehrig and young Joe DiMaggio powered the team to three more.

But Gehrig is best remembered for the iron-man streak that lasted from 1925-39, when a fatal disease—amyotrophic lateral sclerosis—ended his career prematurely and tugged at the heart string of a nation. Gehrig, finally accorded the recognition that long had eluded him, died two years later.

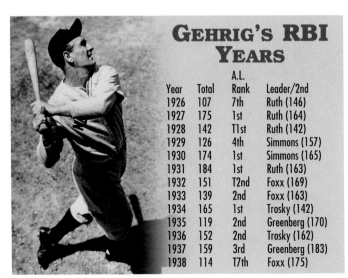

GEHRIG'S RBI YEARS

Year	Total	A.L. Rank	Leader/2nd
1926	107	7th	Ruth (146)
1927	175	1st	Ruth (164)
1928	142	T1st	Ruth (142)
1929	126	4th	Simmons (157)
1930	174	1st	Simmons (165)
1931	184	1st	Ruth (163)
1932	151	T2nd	Foxx (169)
1933	139	2nd	Foxx (163)
1934	165	1st	Trosky (142)
1935	119	2nd	Greenberg (170)
1936	152	2nd	Trosky (162)
1937	159	3rd	Greenberg (183)
1938	114	T7th	Foxx (175)

CHRISTY 8
MATHEWSON

P *1900-1916: GIANTS, REDS*

He was an unusual combination of finesse, guile and controlled intensity, a baseball artist who turned out pitching masterpieces over the first 17 years of the 20th century. Christy Mathewson was the Greg Maddux of yesteryear and his National League record-tying 373 career victories still stand as testimony to artistic efficiency.

When Mathewson threw his first pitch for John McGraw's New York Giants in the summer of 1900, he provided a breath of fresh air for the rough-and-tumble game that scared away the more genteel, educated class of would-be fan. Matty, a product of Bucknell University, helped change baseball's image and he did it without the power style that characterized most pitchers of the era.

"You could sit in a chair and catch Matty," said former Giants catcher Chief Meyers and, indeed, the righthanded Mathewson delivered his pitches with an easy overhand motion and pinpoint control. He worked with savvy, seldom walked a batter and spotted pitches, letting fielders do their job. His typical game required 80 to 90 pitches and he seldom topped 100. When in trouble, he turned to his special fadeaway curve—a modern-day screwball that mesmerized both lefthanded and righthanded hitters.

Mathewson, a first-ballot Hall of Fame selection in the charter class of 1936, also mesmerized record keepers with his numbers. He was the workhorse of Giants teams that won five pennants and a World Series from 1904-13—a four-time 30-game winner who set a still-standing modern N.L. record with 37 victories in 1908. His pitching ledger is filled with 20-win seasons (13), ERA titles (5), shutouts (79) and strikeout crowns (4). Matty's three straight 30-win seasons from 1903-05 were matched by only Grover Alexander among 20th century hurlers.

Mathewson is best remembered for two performances—one good, one bad. His three-shutout 1905 World Series effort against Connie Mack's Philadelphia A's has never been duplicated and he was the pitcher who lost to Chicago nemesis Three-Finger Brown in the one-game playoff that decided the infamous 1908 "Merkle's Boner" pennant race.

THE OVER-35 GANG

When Mathewson won a modern National League-record 37 games in 1908, he joined the short list of 35-game winners in the 20th century:

W-L	Pitcher/Team	Year
41-12	Jack Chesbro, Yankees	1904
40-15	Ed Walsh, White Sox	1908
37-11	Christy Mathewson, Giants	1908
36-7	Walter Johnson, Senators	1913
35-8	Joe McGinnity, Giants	1904

"With Johnson, it was brute force.
With Mathewson, it was knowledge and judgment,
perfect control and form.
It was a pleasure to watch him pitch."

CONNIE MACK, 1943

> 66 (Williams) is the most remarkable hitter I ever saw. ... I never saw a hitter who could swing as late as he does and hit the ball as good. 99
>
> BILL DICKEY
> THE SPORTING NEWS, 1946

TED 9 WILLIAMS

OF ◆ *1939-1942, 1946-1960: RED SOX*

Nobody was more dedicated to the art of putting bat on ball than Ted Williams, a human hitting machine equipped with near-perfect eyesight, lightning reflexes, powerful forearms and unnerving patience. The "Splendid Splinter" also came with a heavy dose of arrogance and self-confidence, the most conspicuous traits of a baseball maverick who terrorized American League pitchers from 1939-60.

If Williams wasn't the greatest pure hitter of all time, he certainly was of his era. A lefthanded swinger, he stood erect, hands holding bat in a vice-like grip, straight up and close to his left shoulder. Williams would throw his gangly body forward, always keeping his hands back, until a blurry, split-second swing whipped out another line drive. Always a perfectionist, Williams refused to swing at a bad pitch, a discipline that made him one of the three most-walked hitters in history and a 12-time leader in on-base percentage.

But the self-discipline that so defined Williams the hitter often was lost on Williams the man. Quick-tempered, cocky, opinionated and independent, the sensitive Williams, a sometimes-erratic defender in left field, fought career-long battles against critical sportswriters and fickle Boston fans. His feud with the media might have cost him three MVP awards—in 1941 when he posted baseball's last .400 average (.406) but lost out to New York's Joe DiMaggio; in 1942 and '47 when he won two Triple Crowns but lost out in voting to Yankees Joe Gordon and DiMaggio.

The Williams bottom line still is filled with superlatives—two MVPs, six batting crowns, 2,654 hits, a .344 average, 18 All-Star Games, 521 home runs, four homer titles and five RBI crowns—numbers that could have been considerably higher if he had not lost four prime seasons to military service during World War II and the Korean War.

Williams never played for a World Series champion, but he did retire with dramatic flair in 1960, hitting a home run at Fenway Park in his final at-bat.

A NOT-SO-DISTANT SECOND

How Williams compared to American League MVP winners Joe DiMaggio and Joe Gordon in his three most memorable seasons—his .406 campaign of 1941 and his Triple Crown seasons of 1942 and '47:

1941	R	H	HR	RBI	Avg.
DiMaggio	122	193	30	125	.357
Williams	135	185	37	120	.406
1942	R	H	HR	RBI	Avg.
Gordon	88	173	18	103	.322
Williams	141	186	36	137	.356
1947	R	H	HR	RBI	Avg.
DiMaggio	97	168	20	97	.315
Williams	125	181	32	114	.343

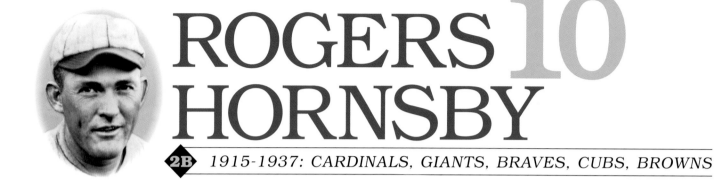

ROGERS HORNSBY 10

2B *1915-1937: CARDINALS, GIANTS, BRAVES, CUBS, BROWNS*

As a man, Rogers Hornsby was truculent, aloof and a self-absorbed loner who always spoke his mind and seldom worried about the consequences. As a ballplayer, "Rajah" lived up to his nickname—proud, brash and majestic, especially when he stepped to the plate and let his never-silent bat do the talking.

Hornsby possessed cat-like reflexes and sprinter speed, qualities that doubled his impact as a devastating hitter and one of the best-fielding second basemen of the first half century. He stood deep in the box and rocketed line drives to all fields, a hitting style that helped him string together the best six-season offensive stretch in baseball history.

Playing for the St. Louis Cardinals, Hornsby posted averages of .370, .397, .401, .384, .424 (the highest average of the century) and .403 from 1920-25, winning six straight National League batting titles, two Triple Crowns and adulation as the greatest righthanded hitter of the modern era. He also led the N.L. in slugging and on-base percentage in each of those campaigns while topping the charts four times in RBIs and hits, three times in runs and twice in homers. Hornsby was, simply stated, prolific.

In 1926, he doubled as player/manager of the Cardinals and led them to their first N.L. pennant and World Series championship. But that was the season Hornsby's confrontational style wore thin and he was shipped to the New York Giants for Frank Frisch and Jimmy Ring in a shocking December trade that transformed him into a hired gun who could always be counted on to post big numbers and defy authority figures he seemed to resent.

Over the rest of Hornsby's 23-year playing career, he changed uniforms five times, won his seventh batting title (with the Boston Braves in 1928) and helped the Chicago Cubs win a 1929 pennant. He finished his career in 1937 after five years as player/manager of the lowly St. Louis Browns, retiring with 2,930 hits and the second-highest average in history (.358).

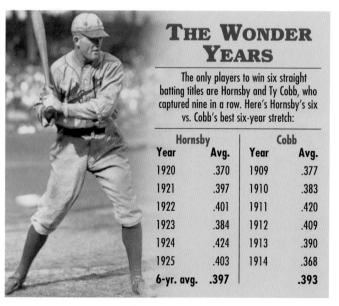

THE WONDER YEARS

The only players to win six straight batting titles are Hornsby and Ty Cobb, who captured nine in a row. Here's Hornsby's six vs. Cobb's best six-year stretch:

Hornsby		Cobb	
Year	Avg.	Year	Avg.
1920	.370	1909	.377
1921	.397	1910	.383
1922	.401	1911	.420
1923	.384	1912	.409
1924	.424	1913	.390
1925	.403	1914	.368
6-yr. avg.	.397		.393

"I don't like to sound egotistical, but every time I stepped up to the plate with a bat in my hands, I couldn't help but feel sorry for the pitcher."

ROGERS HORNSBY, 1953

STAN MUSIAL 11

He had the menacing look of a cobra—crouched at the hips, legs close together in the back of the box with right heel elevated, bat cocked straight up, eyes peering over the right shoulder in a hypnotic search for a moving target. When the ball arrived, Stan (The Man) Musial uncoiled, driving another hit into his impressive record book.

Musial treated St. Louis fans to 3,630 of them over a 22-year career that touched three decades and produced a .331 average. He also captured the heart of an adoring city with his affable, friendly personality and quick smile—characteristics that would continue to enchant legions of admirers decades after his 1963 retirement.

That smile first was spotted in a 12-game 1941 preview and it became a fixture over his next four seasons (1945 was spent in military service) as the 6-foot, 175-pound right fielder/first baseman powered the Cardinals to four pennants and three World Series championships. He also won two of the seven National League batting titles he would claim.

While Musial was not a Ruthian-type power hitter, careless pitchers paid for their mistakes. He muscled up for 475 career home runs, including five in a memorable 1954 doubleheader against the New York Giants, and finished with 1,377 extra-base hits, second only to Hank Aaron on the all-time list. Musial ranks in the top five of numerous all-time categories, he's one of four players to win three or more N.L. MVP awards and he appeared in a record-tying 24 All-Star Games, hitting a record six All-Star home runs.

His hitting feats are nothing less than extraordinary. Musial led the N.L in doubles eight times, in runs five times and in hits, on-base percentage and slugging percentage six times. But his greatest legacy might have been the goodwill he brought to the game and his enduring rapport with the fans. Musial was living proof that a take-no-prisoners intensity is not necessarily a prerequisite for success.

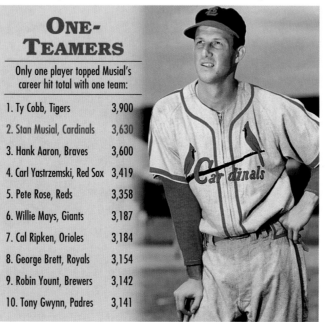

ONE-TEAMERS

Only one player topped Musial's career hit total with one team:

1. Ty Cobb, Tigers	3,900
2. Stan Musial, Cardinals	3,630
3. Hank Aaron, Braves	3,600
4. Carl Yastrzemski, Red Sox	3,419
5. Pete Rose, Reds	3,358
6. Willie Mays, Giants	3,187
7. Cal Ripken, Orioles	3,184
8. George Brett, Royals	3,154
9. Robin Yount, Brewers	3,142
10. Tony Gwynn, Padres	3,141

"No man has ever been a perfect ballplayer. Stan Musial, however, is the closest thing to perfection in the game today. ... He's certainly one of the great hitters of all time."

TY COBB, 1953

JOE 12
DiMAGGIO

Aloof and mysterious, graceful and dignified, the very essence of Joe DiMaggio defied his status as an American icon. But years after he retired from a Hall of Fame career, years after his marriage to movie star Marilyn Monroe had ended, years after his name had been immortalized in song by Simon and Garfunkel and in television lore by Mr. Coffee commercials, DiMaggio main-

tained his status as a genuine hero.

That unwanted superstardom was thrust upon a 21-year-old do-everything center fielder when he made a spectacular 1936 debut with the New York Yankees, batting .323 with 29 home runs, 125 RBIs and an A.L. rookie-record 132 runs scored. It was love at first sight for New York fans, who immediately accorded DiMaggio the hero status passed down from Babe Ruth and Lou Gehrig. Over a 13-season career interrupted by three years of military service, "Joltin' Joe" reciprocated by leading the Yankees to 10 American League pennants and nine World Series championships.

Everything about the 6-foot-2 Californian suggested class. DiMaggio roamed the expansive center field pasture at Yankee Stadium like a gazelle, fearlessly attacked pitchers with his lashing righthanded swing and quietly personified the team-first philoso-

phy of the Yankees. Even his stance—feet spread wide, bat held straight and motionless—was distinctive and everybody marveled at his instinctive baserunning ability.

DiMaggio, a national symbol for Italian-American success, handled his superstar burden with quiet dignity. He fought through numerous injuries to compile a .325 career average, win two batting titles and top 100 RBIs nine times. His 1941 record 56-game hitting streak is a legendary feat and he shares the A.L. record for MVP awards with three. Amazingly, the two-time home run champion posted almost as many career homers (361) as strikeouts (369).

DiMaggio, who was selected to play for the A.L. All-Star team in each of his 13 seasons, passed on his center field aura to Mickey Mantle after his 1951 retirement. That aura lives on today, like the Yankee World Series dynasty he helped create.

56 AND COUNTING

Some quick facts and figures from DiMaggio's record 56-game hitting streak in 1941:

Average	.408
At-Bats	223
Runs	56
Hits	91
Doubles	16
Triples	4
Home Runs	15
RBIs	55
1st Hit	May 15
Last Hit	July 16

" Where have you gone, Joe DiMaggio?
A nation turns its lonely eyes to you. "

SIMON AND GARFUNKEL, 1967

GROVER 13
ALEXANDER

P ▶ *1911-1930: PHILLIES, CUBS, CARDINALS*

Grover Cleveland Alexander spent 20 major league seasons creating two legends: an on-field master who posted a National League-record-tying 373 career victories, and an off-field drifter who battled alcoholism and other problems to an inglorious end. The control that so defined his pitching success was notably absent in a demonic vice that defined and overpowered his personal life.

The slim 6-foot-1 Alexander, a Nebraska farm boy, burst upon the big-league scene in 1911 with the greatest rookie performance in history— a 28-13 record and 2.57 ERA for the Philadelphia Phillies. His smooth, effortless, three-quarters and sidearm motions mesmerized opposing hitters and his laser-like fastball and sweeping curves were delivered with pinpoint precision.

"Alex had the most perfect control of any pitcher I ever saw," Hall of Fame outfielder Max Carey once said, and he was a fast worker who operated with unerring instinct and confidence. Alexander's 1915, '16 and '17 seasons were masterpieces. He was 31-10, 33-12 and 30-13; his ERAs were 1.22, 1.55 and 1.83; he led the N.L. in innings and strikeouts all three years; and he posted 36 shutouts, including a still-standing record of 16 in 1916. The 1915 Phillies won the franchise's first pennant

and Alex recorded their only World Series win in a five-game loss to Boston.

Alexander's seven-season, 190-victory Philadelphia record, which included 61 of his 90 career shutouts (second all-time), was carved out while pitching in the Phillies' tiny Baker Bowl. He followed Philadelphia with 12 less-spectacular but still-productive N.L. seasons in Chicago and St. Louis after spending most of the 1918 campaign on the front line during World War II.

Alexander is best remembered for one dramatic 1926 performance when, at age 39 and reportedly hung over after a night of revelry, he entered the seventh inning of World Series Game 7 with two out and the bases loaded to face New York Yankees slugger Tony Lazzeri. He struck Lazzeri out, preserving the Cardinals' 3-2 lead, and pitched the final two innings to preserve St. Louis' first World Series championship.

OLD PETE VS. BIG SIX

Alexander and Christy Mathewson, who share the N.L record with 373 career wins, are the only pitchers to win 30 games in three straight seasons:

ALEXANDER

Year	W	L	IP	ShO	ERA
1915	31	10	376.1	12	1.22
1916	33	12	389.0	16	1.55
1917	30	13	388.0	8	1.83

MATHEWSON

Year	W	L	IP	ShO	ERA
1903	30	13	366.1	3	2.26
1904	33	12	367.2	4	2.03
1905	31	9	338.2	8	1.28

66 He made me want to throw my bat
away when I went to the plate. He
fed me pitches I couldn't hit. 99

JOHNNY EVERS
FORMER CUBS SECOND BASEMAN

HONUS 14 WAGNER

SS *1897-1917: LOUISVILLE, PIRATES*

T he 5-foot-11, 200-pound gorilla-like frame featured a thick, massive chest, long arms and legs so bowed you could roll a barrel between them. Hall of Fame pitcher Lefty Gomez, who enjoyed the good fortune of never having to face Honus Wagner, once quipped, "He was the only ballplayer who could tie his shoelaces without bending down."

Wagner, a.k.a. the Flying Dutchman, was nobody's prototypical athlete. But when he stepped onto a baseball field, he magically transformed into one of the most versatile players in the history of the game. Wagner could pitch or play any infield or outfield position, but he is most fondly remembered as the first great shortstop of the 20th century and the National League's most proficient batsman of his era.

Wagner was to Pittsburgh what Ty Cobb was to Detroit and Babe Ruth to New York. From 1900-17, he enchanted Pirates fans with his deceptive range, the oversized, shovel-like hands that sucked every ground ball into his undersized mitt and a rifle arm that allowed him to make plays from deep in the hole—and beyond. Outstanding contact hitters of the dead-ball era knew better than to hit the ball to the left side of Pittsburgh's infield.

Offensively, Wagner overmatched the usually dominant pitchers of his era. His career total of 3,420 hits ranks sixth all-time and his .327 average produced a National League record-tying eight batting titles. He led the league in doubles seven times, runs twice, RBIs five times, extra-base hits seven times, triples three times, slugging six times and he even captured five stolen base crowns. There was, simply, nothing Wagner couldn't do.

Not surprisingly, the Dutchman's proficiency sparked the Pirates to four N.L. pennants and a 1909 World Series victory over Cobb's Tigers. When the first Hall of Fame class was selected in 1936, Wagner and Ruth tied for second in the voting, behind only Cobb and ahead of Christy Mathewson and Walter Johnson.

THE 10-YEAR ITCH

Wagner was the greatest hitter of the century's first decade, winning seven of his eight batting championships before 1910. Ten other players captured four or more titles in a decade, with Tony Gwynn doing it twice:

No.	Player	Decade
9	Ty Cobb	1910s
7	Honus Wagner	1900s
7	Rogers Hornsby	1920s
6	Rod Carew	1970s
5	Wade Boggs	1980s
4	Napoleon Lajoie	1900s
4	Harry Heilmann	1920s
4	Ted Williams	1940s
4	Stan Musial	1950s
4	Roberto Clemente	1960s
4	Tony Gwynn	1980s
4	Tony Gwynn	1990s

"I hold out for Hans Wagner as the greatest of them all. Wagner was a great ballplayer at 20. He was still a great ballplayer at 43. In all my career, I never saw such a versatile player."

JOHN MCGRAW
THE SPORTING NEWS, 1931

" If (Clemens) is not the best, I'd
hate to see who is. When they
made the mold for pitchers, they
made him. He's the perfect pitcher. **"**

DAN PLESAC

MAJOR LEAGUE PITCHER
THE SPORTING NEWS, 1988

ROGER 15 CLEMENS

P *1984-PRESENT: RED SOX, BLUE JAYS, YANKEES, ASTROS*

He's cocky, intensely focused and the master of his baseball universe. And he's explosive, much like the fastball he has blown past hitters for 22 major league seasons. When the sometimes-volatile, always-confident Roger Clemens pitches, everybody listens—and that sound they hear is another pitch whistling through the strike zone and into the catcher's mitt.

Finesse is not a quality associated with the 6-4, 235-pound righthander who embraces the very essence of his "Rocket" nickname. Clemens is raw power, a finely tuned strikeout machine driven by strong legs, a resilient arm and an intense competitive fire. When the big Texan is at his best with a 96-mph fastball, a late-diving splitter and a mid-80s slider, he is close to unhittable. Seattle batters found that out in 1986 when Clemens mowed them down in a record-setting 20-strikeout masterpiece; Detroit hitters felt the same way 10 years later when he matched that remarkable strikeout feat.

Clemens' resume is filled with evidence of pitching mastery: six 20-win seasons, a 3.12 ERA, 341 wins, a .665 winning percentage and 4,502 strikeouts, a career total topped only by Nolan Ryan. Adding to the dominance are those amazing Cy Young Awards—seven won with four teams. At 42, Clemens won the last of those in 2004 while making his National League debut with his hometown Houston Astros; three others came in 13 seasons with Boston, two in as many seasons in Toronto and one in five years with the New York Yankees.

Clemens, a nine-time All-Star, posted his first big season in 1986—the year after he underwent shoulder surgery. He swept A.L. Cy Young and MVP honors while finishing 24-4 and leading the Red Sox to a pennant. But the Clemens mystique grew with age. He forged 21- and 20-win seasons in his only two years with the young Blue Jays, and he pitched for two World Series champions in New York, where he posted a 20-3 mark in 2001. His 18-4 debut with the Astros put icing on his Hall of Fame credentials.

TWO-TIMERS

Clemens is one of nine pitchers to win Cy Young and MVP awards in the same season:

Pitcher/Team	Yr.
Don Newcombe, Dodgers	1956
Sandy Koufax, Dodgers	1963
Denny McLain, Tigers	1968
Bob Gibson, Cardinals	1968
Vida Blue, Athletics	1971
Rollie Fingers, Athletics	1981
Willie Hernandez, Tigers	1984
Roger Clemens, Red Sox	1986
Dennis Eckersley, Athletics	1992

CY16 YOUNG

P 1890-1911: CLEVELAND, ST. LOUIS, RED SOX, INDIANS, BRAVES

His name is synonymous with masterful pitching and career success often is measured by an award bearing his name. If Cy Young wasn't the greatest pitcher in baseball history, he certainly was the game's most consistently prolific hurler and the first one destined for immortality that transcends what he accomplished on the field.

Denton True Young, a Civil War baby boomer who delivered his first pitches with oranges on his father's Ohio farm, burst upon the major league scene with the Cleveland Spiders in 1890 and began piecing together a 22-year pitching legacy that would include five 30-win seasons and 15 with 20 or more. For turn-of-the-century hitters, the 6-foot-2, 210-pound righthander was a magician who could work every other day and seemed to sense their every weakness.

Young's secret was a photographic memory that allowed him to mentally chart every batter and an assortment of pitches that kept them guessing and flailing weakly at his pinpoint deliveries. He used four motions, all of which started with his back to the plate, and his fastball was among the fastest of the period. He threw two curves, a big breaker from an overhand motion and a "swerve" that was delivered sidearm. A superb

changeup also was part of an act that baffled hitters until 1911.

The amazing thing about Young was his consistency. In the 19-year stretch from 1891-1909, he dipped below 18 wins only once and 300 innings three times. His career bridged baseball's 50-foot pitching distance and such turn-of-the-century stars as Christy Mathewson, Walter Johnson and Ty Cobb. He threw three no-hitters, one a 1904 perfect game, while pitching 12 seasons with Cleveland, St. Louis and Boston in the N.L.; 10 with Boston and Cleveland in the A.L.

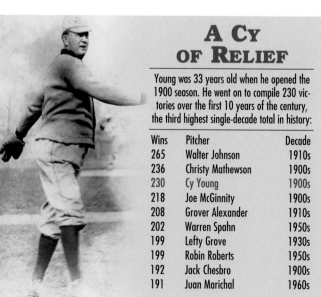

A CY OF RELIEF

Young was 33 years old when he opened the 1900 season. He went on to compile 230 victories over the first 10 years of the century, the third highest single-decade total in history:

Wins	Pitcher	Decade
265	Walter Johnson	1910s
236	Christy Mathewson	1900s
230	Cy Young	1900s
218	Joe McGinnity	1900s
208	Grover Alexander	1910s
202	Warren Spahn	1950s
199	Lefty Grove	1930s
199	Robin Roberts	1950s
192	Jack Chesbro	1900s
191	Juan Marichal	1960s

Young is most celebrated for his career-record 511 wins, but just as amazing are his career marks for innings (7,356), 300-inning seasons (16) and complete games (749). He also was the starter and loser for the Red Sox in baseball's first World Series game in 1903.

> **I don't expect to see a second Cy Young. Men who combine his coordinated talents of mind and arm are not born often.**
>
> JOHN McGRAW

JIMMIE FOXX 17

There was nothing quite like a Jimmie Foxx home run: powerful, muscular arms whipping a 37-ounce bat into a pitch with incredible speed; ball rocketing from home plate to places beyond even faster. Blink and you might miss the split-second experience. Watch closely and you might even see the vapor trail.

Unlike a Babe Ruth homer that was majestic and almost serene, a Foxx homer was brute force. Such power generated from a 5-foot-11, 195-pound former Maryland farmboy, who emerged in 1925 as the srongman of Connie Mack's Philadelphia Athletics lineup and the first serious challenger to Ruth's power-hitting dominance. Foxx was a menacing figure when he stood at the plate with a fixed glare, waving the bat with biceps that bulged from sleeves cut deliberately short.

From his breakthrough 1929 season with the A's through 1940, his fifth season with the Boston Red Sox, Foxx never failed to hit 30 homers or drive in 100 runs, a remarkable 12-year stretch. He also led the A's to three pennants and two World Series championships, won two batting titles, topped the 50-homer plateau twice and won a 1933 Triple Crown with his .356 average, 48 homers and 163 RBIs. But 1932 was Foxx's masterpiece, his brush with baseball immortality.

That was the season "Double X" batted .364, drove in 169 runs and exploded for 58 home runs, just two short of Ruth's 1927 single-season record. It earned him the first of consecutive MVP awards and became the signature season in a 20-year career that produced 534 home runs, a total that ranked second all-time to Ruth for many years. Foxx, who teamed with Ted Williams in the Boston lineup after leaving Philadelphia in 1936, ended his career in 1945 with a .325 average and a record-tying 13 100-RBI seasons.

Foxx, a friendly, popular clubhouse figure and a notorious night owl, was much more than a plodding slugger. His defensive versatility allowed managers to use him at catcher, first and third base, and in the outfield with full confidence in his abilities.

FOXX TROT

Foxx holds the record for consecutive 30-homer/100-RBI seasons with 12:

Year	HR	RBI
1929	33	118
1930	37	156
1931	30	120
1932	58	169
1933	48	163
1934	44	130
1935	36	115
1936	41	143
1937	36	127
1938	50	175
1939	35	105
1940	36	119
Avg.	40.3	136.7

66 In my long association with players in the big leagues, I never saw a player with more natural ability than Double X. He had everything you could ask for in a player. 99

JOE CRONIN
THE SPORTING NEWS, 1955

> 66 Bench is the greatest athlete who ever has played the game. It's almost pitiful that one man should have so much talent. 99
>
> SPARKY ANDERSON
> THE SPORTING NEWS, 1970

JOHNNY BENCH 18

C *1967-1983: REDS*

It might not seem fair, but Johnny Bench is the standard by which catchers will be judged forever. From the rock-solid 210-pound frame that guarded home plate like a stone wall to the cannon-size arm that bewildered baserunners with laser-like throws to second base, Bench gave future generations of catchers a floor plan for Hall of Fame success.

From the first moment of his 1967 debut with the Cincinnati Reds, there was little doubt about the impact he would have on the game. Bench's incredible tools—the arm, the huge hands that could hold seven baseballs at one time, the cat-like quickness—allowed him to play the way no other catcher had dared. Not only did he do everything better than his predecessors, he redefined the position with his one-handed catching style, the one-handed sweep tag that shocked veteran baseball people and the helmet and over-sized glove that became part of every catcher's equipment.

Bench could dominate games from behind the plate, where he earned 10 Gold Gloves and set then-National League records with 9,260 putouts and 10,110 total chances while compiling a .990 fielding percentage. Or he could dominate with a bat that produced six

100-RBI seasons, three N.L. RBI titles and a pair of home run crowns (45 in 1970, 40 in '72). Of his 389 career homers, 327 came as a catcher—third behind Mike Piazza and Carlton Fisk on the all-time list.

Bench, the 1968 Rookie of the Year, is best remembered as the power behind a Big Red Machine that ran roughshod over the N.L. in the 1970s, winning four pennants and two World Series. He also captured two MVP awards in the decade while anchoring 1975 and '76 teams that often are ranked among the best in history.

Bench, a proud Oklahoman who played through 10 broken bones in his feet and numerous knee problems throughout his 17-year career, also was fast enough to record double-figure stolen base totals twice. He punctuated his outstanding career with 12 All-Star Game appearances.

CATCHING UP WITH JOHNNY

Bench was the only catcher in the 20th century to lead his league in home runs, and one of four to lead his league in RBIs:

League Leader, Year	HR	RBI
Roy Campanella, 1953		142
Johnny Bench, 1970	45	148
Johnny Bench, 1972	40	125
Johnny Bench, 1974		129
Gary Carter, 1984		*106
Darren Daulton, 1992		109

*Tied for league lead

MICKEY MANTLE 19

When he cut his Oklahoma ties in 1949, he was called the "Commerce Comet," and when he retired from baseball 20 seasons later he was known affectionately, simply, as "The Mick." In between, a naive country boy named Mickey Mantle rose to prominence as a national icon and the centerpiece of a New York Yankees dynasty that captured 12 American

League pennants and seven World Series championships over a glorious 14-year span.

The husky, blond, switch-hitting 19-year-old with blacksmith arms, sprinter speed and an unassuming, home-spun charm arrived in 1951 as the heir apparent to center fielder Joe DiMaggio, a New York idol who was playing his final season. In the Babe Ruth-Lou Gehrig-DiMaggio tradition that had helped the Yankees achieve baseball superiority for three decades, Mantle, 200 pounds of unprecedented power from both sides of the plate, eventually won over fans with his tape-measure home runs and an almost-mystical aura that would transcend his 18-year major league career.

Mantle, who played in 16 All-Star Games, was plagued by a series of early knee problems that compromised his all-around skills and prematurely triggered a decline, but

his power-hitting feats remain legendary. Fans still talk about the 565-foot Mantle blast that left Washington's Griffith Park in 1953 and the moon-shot homer that almost cleared Yankee Stadium's right field facade 10 years later. And not only were his home runs long, they were frequent.

Two times Mantle topped the 50 plateau—in 1956 when he won a Triple Crown (.353, 52 homers, 130 RBIs) and in 1961 when he hit 54 while joining teammate Roger Maris in the chase of Ruth's single-season record—en route to a career total of 536. And 10 times he complemented that power with .300-plus averages that helped him earn three MVP awards.

But Mantle's greatest legacy was written in the 12 World Series in which he set numerous fall classic records, including home runs (18), RBIs (40), runs (42), extra-base hits (26) and total bases (123).

POWER AND FINESSE

Mantle (1956) and Jimmie Foxx (1938) are the only players to hit 50 or more home runs during a season in which they won a batting title. Mantle also earned an A.L. Triple Crown.

	FOXX	MANTLE
Hits	197	188
Runs	139	132
Homers	50	52
RBIs	175	130
Average	.349	.353

> "He can do everything. He hits the ball a mile, he catches so easily he might as well be in a rocking chair, throws like a bullet. Bill Dickey isn't as good a catcher."

WALTER JOHNSON

JOSH 20 GIBSON

C 1930-1946: NEGRO LEAGUES

He was to Negro League baseball what Babe Ruth was to the all-white game of his era. The Josh Gibson legend is filled with stories of long, longer and longest home runs, other incredible batting feats and testimonials from long-time teammates and supporters that he was at least equal to the Sultan of Swat, maybe even better.

The baseball world will never know for sure because Gibson, a barrel-chested 220-pound catcher, never had the chance to test his skills in the major leagues. But those who watched him play from 1930-46 for the Homestead Grays and Pittsburgh Crawfords described an intimidating righthanded hitter who seldom struck out and powered mammoth home runs from a flat-footed stance with a simple flick of his wrists.

Gibson hit for high averages, too, but discussions about the big Georgian always focus on his legendary power. He was the king of 600-foot homers with signature blows that reportedly sailed out of such ballparks as Yankee Stadium, the Polo Grounds, Griffith Stadium and Comiskey Park. His upper-body strength was incredible; his batting marks and home run totals (a reported 75 in one season, 962 in his career)

were hard to believe. And when he wasn't winning Negro League home run titles, he was amazing fans in Mexico and the Dominican Republic with his hitting feats.

Gibson, a wide-smiling quiet man with broad shoulders and thick arms, also was an outstanding rifle-arm catcher, once described by pitching great Walter Johnson as better than New York Yankees contemporary Bill Dickey. Other major league players who competed against Gibson and various other Negro League stars during offseason barnstorming games were equally impressed.

Sadly, Gibson was just 35 years old and still active when he suffered a cerebral hemorrhage and died suddenly in January 1947, a few months before Jackie Robinson would gain national attention by breaking baseball's color barrier with the Brooklyn Dodgers.

THE BEST OF THE BEST

Negro League pitching great Satchel Paige named the five toughest hitters he had ever faced in a 1953 story that was printed in Collier's magazine:

1. Josh Gibson

2. Charley Gehringer

3. Larry Doby

4. Joe DiMaggio

5. Ted Williams

SATCHEL 21 PAIGE

P *1926-1951: NEGRO LEAGUES; 1948-1953, 1965: INDIANS, BROWNS, ATHLETICS*

If Satchel Paige wasn't the best pitcher in history, he might have been the most colorful. Enthusiastic, outlandish and endearing, he was a relentless showman who always made baseball fun for the multitudes who flocked to parks to see him pitch over the better part of four decades, most of which he spent dominating the 1920s, '30s and '40s Negro Leagues.

Paige was a physical anomaly who tested his rubber arm to the limit in working an estimated 2,600 games, as many as 200 in several year-round seasons. The lanky 6-foot-4 righthander delivered his blazing fastball with a windmill delivery and perfect control, often juicing up expectant fans by following through on crazy predictions and stunts (like pulling teammates off the field and then striking out the side). Ever the baseball ambassador, Paige filled ballparks for the struggling Negro Leagues while drifting from town to town and team to team, but his reputation really spread during seasons with the Pittsburgh Crawfords and Kansas City Monarchs.

It was with the Crawfords that Paige formed a Hall of Fame battery with Josh Gibson, the one black star who could almost match his popularity. And fans read stories about barnstorming games against major lea-guers in which Paige outdueled such pitching stars as Dizzy Dean and Bob Feller. When an aging Paige finally was allowed to enter the white major leagues, curious fans flocked to see him pitch. Paige's fastball was dominant through most of his Negro League days, but he tantalized major leaguers with his off-speed deliveries as a 42-year-old Cleveland rookie (1948) and successful St. Louis Browns reliever (1951-53). Paige even made a curtain call in 1965 for Charlie Finley's Kansas City Athletics, working three scoreless innings against the Boston Red Sox—at age 59.

Although Paige did not get to test his skills at the major league level until well after his prime, he still became an American folk hero who charmed teammates and audiences with self-effacing humor and home-spun stories. And, of course, that room-lighting smile.

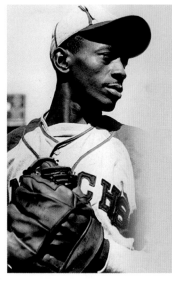

STAYING YOUNG

This was Paige's advice for a long, active life:

1. Avoid fried meats, which angry up the blood.

2. If your stomach disputes you, lie down and pacify it with cool thoughts.

3. Keep the juices flowing by jangling around gently as you move.

4. Go very light on the vices, such as carrying on in society. The social ramble ain't restful.

5. Avoid running at all times.

6. Don't look back. Something might be gaining on you.

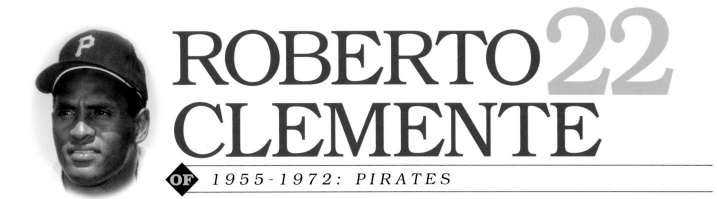

ROBERTO CLEMENTE 22

He strutted through 18 major league seasons like a high-strung thoroughbred and gained baseball immortality in a tragic career-ending death while acting as a life-sustaining humanitarian. Proud, honest, intense, sensitive and incredibly talented: Adjectives simply oozed from the sometimes-complicated persona of Roberto Clemente.

The Pittsburgh Pirates great, who learned the game on the sandlots of his native Puerto Rico, was baseball's prototypical right fielder from 1955-72—a defensive machine built around speed, razor-sharp instincts and an arm that terrorized baserunners throughout the National League. He patrolled the vast right field pasture at Forbes Field for most of his career, defiantly staking his claim to greatness with 12 Gold Gloves and defensive comparisons to outfield contemporary Willie Mays.

Clemente's hitting style was unorthodox, but effective enough to produce four batting titles, an MVP award and 15 All-Star Game invitations. A 5-foot-11, 180-pound specimen with chiseled features and quick wrists, he stood away from the plate and kept hands and bat cocked until the last possible second, seemingly pulling line drives right out of the catcher's mitt with an inside-out swing. He was a notorious bad-ball hitter who posted a .317 average while leading the Pirates to two World Series titles.

Clemente, a chronic complainer about aches and pains that never seemed to affect his play, batted .317 with 29 homers and 119 RBIs in his MVP 1966 season and won batting titles with such averages as .329, .339, .351 and .357. But Pittsburgh fans best remember Clemente's 12-hit, two-homer, .414 flourish that drove the team to a 1971 World Series win over Baltimore.

Clemente never forgot his roots and was revered in Puerto Rico. He was part of a team flying relief supplies to earthquake-ravaged Nicaragua on December 31, 1972, when the small aircraft exploded and crashed into the ocean. His death came only a few months after he had recorded his 3,000th hit and prompted a special election that gave him distinction as baseball's first Hispanic Hall of Famer.

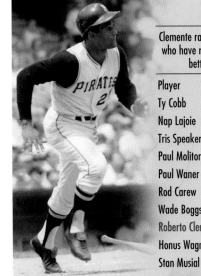

PITT BULL

Clemente ranks last on a list of the 25 post-1900 players who have recorded 3,000 career hits, but he fares a lot better when you compute hits per game:

Player	Hits	Games	Avg.
Ty Cobb	4,189	3,035	1.38
Nap Lajoie	3,242	2,475	1.31
Tris Speaker	3,514	2,789	1.26
Paul Molitor	3,319	2,683	1.237
Paul Waner	3,152	2,549	1.236
Rod Carew	3,053	2,469	1.236
Wade Boggs	3,010	2,440	1.2336
Roberto Clemente	3,000	2,433	1.2330
Honus Wagner	3,420	2,794	1.22
Stan Musial	3,630	3,026	1.20

WARREN 23 SPAHN

P 1942, 1946-1965: BRAVES, METS, GIANTS

S tan Musial called him "an artist with imagination." The Brooklyn Dodgers once named their new pitching machine, "The Warren Spahn." Other National League hitters simply flailed helplessly at his wide assortment of strategically placed pitches for 21 major league seasons and then retired quietly to their seat on the bench.

That's the effect Spahn had on hitters from 1946-65 as he carved out 363 victories, more than any lefthander in history and the fifth-best total all time. An artist, indeed, but more accurately a pitching scientist who could paint corners with his control and confound batters with tantalizing fastballs, curves, sinkers and screwballs barely out of the strike zone.

Spahn, a 6-footer who posted all but seven of his victories for the Boston and Milwaukee Braves, delivered those pitches from a slow, rock-back motion that fueled a high, fluid leg kick and a machine-like over-hand delivery. The hitter looked for the ball amid the illusion of flailing arms and legs. No two pitches looked alike or arrived in the same spot. When Spahnie was sharp, games were fast and the results predictable.

Never more so than in the 17-year stretch from 1947-63, when

Spahn reached the 20-win plateau 13 times and never failed to top 245 innings. He was a workhorse ("Spahn and Sain and pray for rain") for the 1948 pennant-winning Braves and a Cy Young winner in 1957, when Milwaukee won its only championship. Spahn was 4-3 in three World Series and 363-245 overall in a big-league career that didn't really begin until age 25 because of three years of military service in World War II.

An affable, fun-loving prankster off the field, Spahn was all business on the mound. He also was a model of consistency for two decades. In addition to three ERA titles, four strikeout crowns, 63 career shutouts and seven All-Star Game appearances, Spahn pitched two no-hitters—both after his 39th birthday. He rounded out his impressive resume by hitting 35 career home runs.

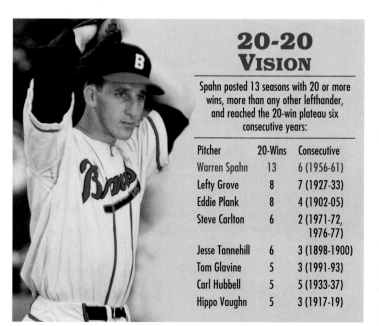

20-20 VISION

Spahn posted 13 seasons with 20 or more wins, more than any other lefthander, and reached the 20-win plateau six consecutive years:

Pitcher	20-Wins	Consecutive
Warren Spahn	13	6 (1956-61)
Lefty Grove	8	7 (1927-33)
Eddie Plank	8	4 (1902-05)
Steve Carlton	6	2 (1971-72, 1976-77)
Jesse Tannehill	6	3 (1898-1900)
Tom Glavine	5	3 (1991-93)
Carl Hubbell	5	5 (1933-37)
Hippo Vaughn	5	3 (1917-19)

“Not only is Warren one of the finest gentlemen in the game, he is also one of the best pitchers I have ever seen.”

CASEY STENGEL, 1959

FRANK 24 ROBINSON

When you cut through all the superlatives, two capture the essence and intensity of the man. Frank Robinson, the self-made star with skinny legs and a big stick, was fearless and inspirational—qualities that earned him the contempt of opponents and the respect and admiration of teammates and fans over a memorable 21-year career.

There was nothing flashy about the in-your-face right fielder who made his first impressions in 1956 when he hit 38 home runs as a 20-year-old Rookie of the Year for Cincinnati. Competing for prestige in an era dominated by such names as Mays, Mantle, Aaron and Clemente, Robinson played with a recklessness, intimidating self-confidence and scowling demeanor that infuriated opponents. He always slid hard, never fraternized with the enemy and wielded a booming bat that produced 586 career homers, sixth on the all-time list.

Even his batting style was confrontational. The 6-foot-1 Robinson crowded the plate like a boxer trying to work inside, daring the pitcher to throw a strike. He crouched, leaned forward, bat pointed upward, and glared toward the mound over an upraised shoulder. Pitchers who greeted his insolence with fastballs to the ribs usually paid a price in subsequent at-bats.

Robinson was an offensive machine for the Reds from 1956-65, winning the 1961 MVP with a 37-homer, 124-RBI performance while leading Cincinnati to a pennant. Reds fans were shocked when man-agement declared Robinson an "old 30" and traded him to Baltimore after a 1965 campaign in which he totaled 33 homers and 113 RBIs.

The young-and-talented Orioles got the outspoken clubhouse leader who would help them win four American League pennants and two World Series in a six-year span. Robinson punctuated that team success with a 1966 Triple Crown (.316, 49, 122) and distinction as the only player to win MVPs in both leagues.

The aging Robinson, who played in 11 All-Star Games, punctuated his career in 1975 with another distinction—he became Cleveland's player-manager and the first black manager in major league history. He celebrated by homering in his first "managerial" at-bat.

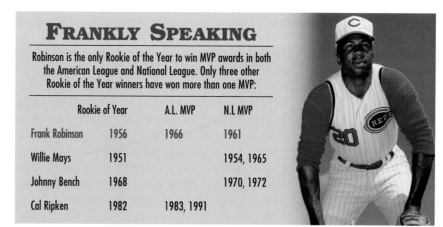

FRANKLY SPEAKING

Robinson is the only Rookie of the Year to win MVP awards in both the American League and National League. Only three other Rookie of the Year winners have won more than one MVP:

	Rookie of Year	A.L. MVP	N.L MVP
Frank Robinson	1956	1966	1961
Willie Mays	1951		1954, 1965
Johnny Bench	1968		1970, 1972
Cal Ripken	1982	1983, 1991	

> " He took terrific talent and made it even better with his intensity. It has never been any secret that anyone who played against Frank hated him while the guys who played with him loved him. "
>
> DAVEY JOHNSON, 1982
> FORMER ORIOLES TEAMMATE

LEFTY 25
GROVE

P 1925-1941: ATHLETICS, RED SOX

Opposing hitters never had a chance against a Lefty Grove fastball, which sailed past them like a meteor unleashed by some other-worldly force. Neither did teammates against the Lefty Grove temper, which erupted into legendary tantrums when things did not go just right over the virulent lefthander's 17-year major league career.

Suffice to say the lean 6-foot-3, 200-pounder was both fast and furious. And incredibly successful, thanks to that uncontrollable intensity he brought to the clubhouse and mound. When he made his big-league debut for Connie Mack's Philadelphia Athletics in 1925, his fastball was as wild as it was fast, and batters stepped into the box with trepidation.

The high-kicking Grove, who would go days without speaking to a teammate because of a defensive lapse, tamed his fastball but never lost the edge his early wildness provided. He enjoyed the first of seven straight 20-win seasons in 1927 and compiled a 152-41 record from 1928-33, a six-year stretch in which the A's won three American League pennants and two World Series.

From 1930-33, he posted records of 28-5, 31-4, 25-10 and 24-8, earned three of his nine career ERA titles and won the last two of seven strikeout titles.

Grove's marquee effort was 1931, when he fashioned the last A.L. 30-win season until 1968. His 2.06 ERA was phenomenal in "a year of the hitter" and he capped his masterpiece with his second straight two-win World Series. In a year in which Lou Gehrig collected 46 homers and 184 RBIs and Babe Ruth amassed 46-163 totals, Grove won MVP honors.

When cost-cutting Mack traded Grove to the Red Sox after the 1933 season, he suffered an arm injury that forced him to transform from a thrower into a pitcher.

Relying on a suddenly improved curveball and sinker, Grove posted 105 Boston victories that gave him a final career mark of 300-141 and a .680 winning percentage that ranks No. 1 all-time among 300-game winners. Those numbers are remarkable when you consider he did not make his big-league debut until age 25.

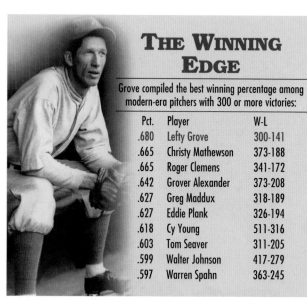

THE WINNING EDGE

Grove compiled the best winning percentage among modern-era pitchers with 300 or more victories:

Pct.	Player	W-L
.680	Lefty Grove	300-141
.665	Christy Mathewson	373-188
.665	Roger Clemens	341-172
.642	Grover Alexander	373-208
.627	Greg Maddux	318-189
.627	Eddie Plank	326-194
.618	Cy Young	511-316
.603	Tom Seaver	311-205
.599	Walter Johnson	417-279
.597	Warren Spahn	363-245

> "It's hard to believe anyone could throw harder than Lefty Grove. I could never pull Grove until the tailend of his career. I'd go up there telling myself I was going to swing the minute he let it go. I'd still hit a ground ball to the third baseman."

CHARLEY GEHRINGER
HALL OF FAME SECOND BASEMAN
THE SPORTING NEWS, 1975

TOP 100 TIMELINE

A chronological breakdown of the Top 100, accompanied by an alphabetical listing and a yearly total of active players. Negro League stars Josh Gibson, Buck Leonard, Cool Papa Bell and Oscar Charleston do not appear because they never played in the major leagues.

Chronological Listing			
Player	Rank	From	To
Cy Young	(16)	1890	1911
Willie Keeler	(77)	1892	1910
Napoleon Lajoie	(31)	1896	1916
Honus Wagner	(14)	1897	1917
Sam Crawford	(87)	1899	1917
Christy Mathewson	(8)	1900	1916
Eddie Plank	(69)	1901	1917
Ed Walsh	(85)	1904	1917
Ty Cobb	(3)	1905	1928
Eddie Collins	(26)	1906	1930
Walter Johnson	(4)	1907	1927
Tris Speaker	(29)	1907	1928
Joe Jackson	(36)	1908	1920
Grover Alexander	(13)	1911	1930
Harry Heilmann	(53)	1914	1932
Babe Ruth	(1)	1914	1935
Rogers Hornsby	(10)	1915	1937
George Sisler	(35)	1915	1930
Frank Frisch	(90)	1919	1937
Pie Traynor	(72)	1920	1937
Lou Gehrig	(7)	1923	1939
Bill Terry	(59)	1923	1936
Charley Gehringer	(46)	1924	1942
Al Simmons	(43)	1924	1944
Mickey Cochrane	(66)	1925	1937
Jimmie Foxx	(17)	1925	1945
Lefty Grove	(25)	1925	1941
Mel Ott	(42)	1926	1947
Paul Waner	(63)	1926	1945
Bill Dickey	(56)	1928	1946
Carl Hubbell	(45)	1928	1943
Chuck Klein	(92)	1928	1944
Dizzy Dean	(88)	1930	1947
Lefty Gomez	(75)	1930	1943
Hank Greenberg	(38)	1930	1947
Joe Medwick	(81)	1932	1948
Joe DiMaggio	(12)	1936	1951
Bob Feller	(37)	1936	1956
Ted Williams	(9)	1939	1960
Stan Musial	(11)	1941	1963
Warren Spahn	(23)	1942	1965
Yogi Berra	(40)	1946	1965
Ralph Kiner	(91)	1946	1955
Jackie Robinson	(44)	1947	1956
Duke Snider	(86)	1947	1964
Roy Campanella	(49)	1948	1957
Satchel Paige	(21)	1948	1965
Robin Roberts	(76)	1948	1966
Whitey Ford	(52)	1950	1967
Mickey Mantle	(19)	1951	1968
Willie Mays	(2)	1951	1973
Eddie Mathews	(64)	1952	1968
Ernie Banks	(39)	1953	1971
Al Kaline	(78)	1953	1974
Hank Aaron	(5)	1954	1976
Harmon Killebrew	(71)	1954	1975
Roberto Clemente	(22)	1955	1972
Sandy Koufax	(28)	1955	1966
Brooks Robinson	(82)	1955	1977
Frank Robinson	(24)	1956	1976
Bob Gibson	(33)	1959	1975
Willie McCovey	(55)	1959	1980
Juan Marichal	(73)	1960	1975
Lou Brock	(58)	1961	1979
Carl Yastrzemski	(74)	1961	1983
Gaylord Perry	(98)	1962	1983
Willie Stargell	(83)	1962	1982
Joe Morgan	(61)	1963	1984
Pete Rose	(27)	1963	1986
Steve Carlton	(32)	1965	1988
Jim Palmer	(65)	1965	1984
Nolan Ryan	(41)	1966	1993
Johnny Bench	(18)	1967	1983
Rod Carew	(62)	1967	1985
Reggie Jackson	(48)	1967	1987
Tom Seaver	(34)	1967	1986
Mike Schmidt	(30)	1972	1989
George Brett	(54)	1973	1993
Dave Winfield	(96)	1973	1995
Dennis Eckersley	(99)	1975	1998
Eddie Murray	(80)	1977	1997
Paul Molitor	(100)	1978	1998
Ozzie Smith	(89)	1978	1996
Rickey Henderson	(50)	1979	2003
Cal Ripken	(79)	1981	2001
Wade Boggs	(94)	1982	1999
Tony Gwynn	(57)	1982	2001
Roger Clemens	(15)	1984	2005
Barry Bonds	(6)	1986	2005
Greg Maddux	(51)	1986	2005
Mark McGwire	(84)	1986	2001
Randy Johnson	(60)	1988	2005
Ken Griffey Jr.	(93)	1989	2005
Sammy Sosa	(95)	1989	2005
Alex Rodriguez	(70)	1994	2005
Derek Jeter	(67)	1995	2005

Chronological Listing

Player	Rank	From	To
Cy Young	(16)	1890	1911
Willie Keeler	(77)	1892	1910
Napoleon Lajoie	(31)	1896	1916
Honus Wagner	(14)	1897	1917
Sam Crawford	(87)	1899	1917
Christy Mathewson	(8)	1900	1916
Eddie Plank	(69)	1901	1917
Ed Walsh	(85)	1904	1917
Ty Cobb	(3)	1905	1928
Eddie Collins	(26)	1906	1930
Walter Johnson	(4)	1907	1927
Tris Speaker	(29)	1907	1928
Joe Jackson	(36)	1908	1920
Grover Alexander	(13)	1911	1930
Harry Heilmann	(53)	1914	1932
Babe Ruth	(1)	1914	1935
Rogers Hornsby	(10)	1915	1937
George Sisler	(35)	1915	1930
Frank Frisch	(90)	1919	1937
Pie Traynor	(72)	1920	1937
Lou Gehrig	(7)	1923	1939
Bill Terry	(59)	1923	1936
Charley Gehringer	(46)	1924	1942
Al Simmons	(43)	1924	1944
Mickey Cochrane	(66)	1925	1937
Jimmie Foxx	(17)	1925	1945
Lefty Grove	(25)	1925	1941
Mel Ott	(42)	1926	1947
Paul Waner	(63)	1926	1945
Bill Dickey	(56)	1928	1946
Carl Hubbell	(45)	1928	1943
Chuck Klein	(92)	1928	1944
Dizzy Dean	(88)	1930	1947
Lefty Gomez	(75)	1930	1943
Hank Greenberg	(38)	1930	1947
Joe Medwick	(81)	1932	1948
Joe DiMaggio	(12)	1936	1951
Bob Feller	(37)	1936	1956
Ted Williams	(9)	1939	1960
Stan Musial	(11)	1941	1963
Warren Spahn	(23)	1942	1965
Yogi Berra	(40)	1946	1965
Ralph Kiner	(91)	1946	1955
Jackie Robinson	(44)	1947	1956
Duke Snider	(86)	1947	1964
Roy Campanella	(49)	1948	1957
Satchel Paige	(21)	1948	1965
Robin Roberts	(76)	1948	1966
Whitey Ford	(52)	1950	1967
Mickey Mantle	(19)	1951	1968
Willie Mays	(2)	1951	1973
Eddie Mathews	(64)	1952	1968
Ernie Banks	(39)	1953	1971
Al Kaline	(78)	1953	1974
Hank Aaron	(5)	1954	1976
Harmon Killebrew	(71)	1954	1975
Roberto Clemente	(22)	1955	1972
Sandy Koufax	(28)	1955	1966
Brooks Robinson	(82)	1955	1977
Frank Robinson	(24)	1956	1976
Bob Gibson	(33)	1959	1975
Willie McCovey	(55)	1959	1980
Juan Marichal	(73)	1960	1975
Lou Brock	(58)	1961	1979
Carl Yastrzemski	(74)	1961	1983
Gaylord Perry	(98)	1962	1983
Willie Stargell	(83)	1962	1982
Joe Morgan	(61)	1963	1984
Pete Rose	(27)	1963	1986
Steve Carlton	(32)	1965	1988
Jim Palmer	(65)	1965	1984
Nolan Ryan	(41)	1966	1993
Johnny Bench	(18)	1967	1983
Rod Carew	(62)	1967	1985
Reggie Jackson	(48)	1967	1987
Tom Seaver	(34)	1967	1986
Mike Schmidt	(30)	1972	1989
George Brett	(54)	1973	1993
Dave Winfield	(96)	1973	1995
Dennis Eckersley	(99)	1975	1998
Eddie Murray	(80)	1977	1997
Paul Molitor	(100)	1978	1998
Ozzie Smith	(89)	1978	1996
Rickey Henderson	(50)	1979	2003
Cal Ripken	(79)	1981	2001
Wade Boggs	(94)	1982	1999
Tony Gwynn	(57)	1982	2001
Roger Clemens	(15)	1984	2005
Barry Bonds	(6)	1986	2005
Greg Maddux	(51)	1986	2005
Mark McGwire	(84)	1986	2001
Randy Johnson	(60)	1988	2005
Ken Griffey Jr.	(93)	1989	2005
Sammy Sosa	(95)	1989	2005
Alex Rodriguez	(70)	1994	2005
Derek Jeter	(97)	1995	2005

Alphabetical listing

Player	Rank	From	To
Aaron, Hank	(5)	1954	1976
Alexander, Grover	(13)	1911	1930
Banks, Ernie	(39)	1953	1971
Bench, Johnny	(18)	1967	1983
Berra, Yogi	(40)	1946	1965
Boggs, Wade	(94)	1982	1999
Bonds, Barry	(6)	1986	2005
Brett, George	(54)	1973	1993
Brock, Lou	(58)	1961	1979
Campanella, Roy	(49)	1948	1957
Carew, Rod	(62)	1967	1985
Carlton, Steve	(32)	1965	1988
Clemens, Roger	(15)	1984	2005
Clemente, Roberto	(22)	1955	1972
Cobb, Ty	(3)	1905	1928
Cochrane, Mickey	(66)	1925	1937
Collins, Eddie	(26)	1906	1930
Crawford, Sam	(87)	1899	1917
Dean, Dizzy	(88)	1930	1947
Dickey, Bill	(56)	1928	1946
DiMaggio, Joe	(12)	1936	1951
Eckersley, Dennis	(99)	1975	1998
Feller, Bob	(37)	1936	1956
Ford, Whitey	(52)	1950	1967
Foxx, Jimmie	(17)	1925	1945
Frisch, Frank	(90)	1919	1937
Gehrig, Lou	(7)	1923	1939
Gehringer, Charley	(46)	1924	1942
Gibson, Bob	(33)	1959	1975
Gomez, Lefty	(75)	1930	1943
Greenberg, Hank	(38)	1930	1947
Griffey Jr., Ken	(93)	1989	2005
Grove, Lefty	(25)	1925	1941
Gwynn, Tony	(57)	1982	2001
Heilmann, Harry	(53)	1914	1932
Henderson, Rickey	(50)	1979	2003
Hornsby, Rogers	(10)	1915	1937
Hubbell, Carl	(45)	1928	1943
Jackson, Joe	(36)	1908	1920
Jackson, Reggie	(48)	1967	1987
Jeter, Derek	(97)	1995	2005
Johnson, Randy	(60)	1988	2005
Johnson, Walter	(4)	1907	1927
Kaline, Al	(78)	1953	1974
Keeler, Willie	(77)	1892	1910
Killebrew, Harmon	(71)	1954	1975
Kiner, Ralph	(91)	1946	1955
Klein, Chuck	(92)	1928	1944
Koufax, Sandy	(28)	1955	1966
Lajoie, Napoleon	(31)	1896	1916
Maddux, Greg	(51)	1986	2005
Mantle, Mickey	(19)	1951	1968
Marichal, Juan	(73)	1960	1975
Mathews, Eddie	(64)	1952	1968
Mathewson, Christy	(8)	1900	1916
Mays, Willie	(2)	1951	1973
McCovey, Willie	(55)	1959	1980
McGwire, Mark	(84)	1986	2001
Medwick, Joe	(81)	1932	1948
Molitor, Paul	(100)	1978	1998
Morgan, Joe	(61)	1963	1984
Murray, Eddie	(80)	1977	1997
Musial, Stan	(11)	1941	1963
Ott, Mel	(42)	1926	1947
Paige, Satchel	(21)	1948	1965
Palmer, Jim	(65)	1965	1984
Perry, Gaylord	(98)	1962	1983
Plank, Eddie	(69)	1901	1917
Ripken, Cal	(79)	1981	2001
Roberts, Robin	(76)	1948	1966
Robinson, Brooks	(82)	1955	1977
Robinson, Frank	(24)	1956	1976
Robinson, Jackie	(44)	1947	1956
Rodriguez, Alex	(70)	1994	2005
Rose, Pete	(27)	1963	1986
Ruth, Babe	(1)	1914	1935
Ryan, Nolan	(41)	1966	1993
Schmidt, Mike	(30)	1972	1989
Seaver, Tom	(34)	1967	1986
Simmons, Al	(43)	1924	1944
Sisler, George	(35)	1915	1930
Smith, Ozzie	(89)	1978	1996
Snider, Duke	(86)	1947	1964
Sosa, Sammy	(95)	1989	2005
Spahn, Warren	(23)	1942	1965
Speaker, Tris	(29)	1907	1928
Stargell, Willie	(83)	1962	1982
Terry, Bill	(59)	1923	1936
Traynor, Pie	(72)	1920	1937
Wagner, Honus	(14)	1897	1917
Walsh, Ed	(85)	1904	1917
Waner, Paul	(63)	1926	1945
Williams, Ted	(9)	1939	1960
Winfield, Dave	(96)	1973	1995
Yastrzemski, Carl	(74)	1961	1983
Young, Cy	(16)	1890	1911

2 14 14 16 18 21 21 19 18 20 21 22 24 27 25 27 25 24 24 24 25 24 24 21 20 22 21 22 20 18 20 18 18 18 18 17 18 17 16 15 13 12 9 9 9 8

1950-59 1960-69 1970-79 1980-89 1990-99 2000-05

61

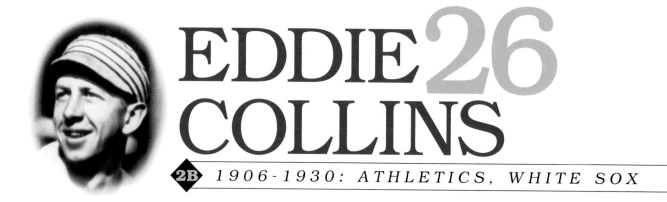

EDDIE 26 COLLINS

2B 1906-1930: ATHLETICS, WHITE SOX

Pound for pound, Eddie Collins might have been the best player in baseball history. Ty Cobb thought he was; so did Collins' former Philadelphia Athletics manager, the esteemed Connie Mack. The 5-foot-9, 175-pound Collins, a graduate of Columbia University, certainly was one of the most cerebral players during his quarter-century reign as the game's best all-around second baseman.

Collins, who began his career in 1906 with Mack's Athletics, covered more ground than early-century contemporary Nap Lajoie, made the double-play pivot more gracefully than late-career rival Rogers Hornsby and was especially adept at retreating into the outfield to pick off potential bloop hits. More than seven decades after his retirement, Collins still owns second base career records for total chances and assists.

The slashing lefthanded hitter was a perfect fit for the dead-ball era in which he spent most of his career and learned to play the game. Collins seldom struck out, posted an impressive .333 average (10 times over .340) and scored lots of runs—1,821 over a career that also produced 3,315 hits. The only reason Collins never won an A.L. batting title was because his career spanned the same period as Cobb.

The speedy Collins, an outstanding bunter and consummate team player, might have been most dangerous on the basepaths. He stole 67 bases in 1909 and 81 a year later en route to a career total of 745, but he is best remembered for his daring dash to the plate in Game 6 of the 1917 World Series with the run that secured a championship for the Chicago White Sox.

Collins also is remembered for other things. He was an innocent member of the 1919 Black Sox team that conspired to throw the World Series; he was a member of Philadelphia's famed $100,000 infield (Stuffy McInnis at first, Collins at second, Jack Barry at shortstop and Home Run Baker at third) in 1913-14; he was a key member of Philadelphia World Series winners in 1910, '11 and '13; and he batted .328 in six fall classics with 42 hits.

ROGERS HORNSBY'S ALL-TIME TEAM

Hornsby selected his all-time team, with Collins at his second base position, for Look magazine in 1952:

1B: George Sisler
2B: Eddie Collins
3B: Pie Traynor
SS: Honus Wagner
LF: Joe Jackson
CF: Tris Speaker
RF: Babe Ruth
C: Mickey Cochrane
   Bill Dickey
RPH: Grover Alexander
   Walter Johnson
LHP: Lefty Grove
   Carl Hubbell

> 66 Eddie Collins was the
> greatest infielder I ever
> saw. He could do
> anything. 99
>
> CONNIE MACK
> THE SPORTING NEWS, 1948

“Pete Rose is an original. He plays the game like nobody else, and his attitude, his enthusiasm, is contagious.”

RULY CARPENTER, 1979

LONGTIME OWNER OF THE PHILLIES

PETE ROSE 27

3B/2B *1963-1986: REDS, PHILLIES, EXPOS* 1B/OF

Arrogant. Cocky. Aggressive. Smart. Intense. Enthusiastic. There aren't enough words to describe the boundless energy Pete Rose brought to baseball for 24 seasons, first as the sparkplug that jump-started Cincinnati's Big Red Machine to World Series titles in 1975 and 1976, and then as the father figure for a 1980 Phillies team that gave Philadelphia its long-awaited first championship.

Rose joined the Reds in 1963 and his perpetual-motion style, whether running to first base after a walk or charging to and from the dugout between innings, quickly earned him the nickname Charlie Hustle—as well as Rookie of the Year honors. He obviously relished the love-hate relationship his take-no-prisoners attitude created with fans. From a crouching, uncoiling stance he slashed line drives all over the field from both sides of the plate, he ran the bases instinctively and aggressively and he prodded opponents into untimely mistakes while inspiring laid-back teammates. Hot dog labels gradually gave way to respect for the three-time N.L. batting champion and 1973 league MVP.

The versatile Rose, who played five infield and outfield positions, seldom missed a game, a durability that allowed him to break one of baseball's most cherished records—Ty Cobb's hit total of 4,191. Rose, a .303 career batter, collected hit No. 3,000 in 1978 for Cincinnati, became the game's second 4,000-hit man in 1984, his only season with Montreal, and stroked No. 4,192, the record-breaker, in a much-ballyhooed 1985 game while serving as player/manager of the Reds, his hometown team. Rose's records of 4,256 hits and 3,562 games played might never be approached.

But the immortality those records should have ensured was cheated by the human side of Rose, who, after months of legal maneuvering, was handed a lifetime ban in 1989 by then-commissioner A. Bartlett Giamatti for betting on baseball games. The ban, which was followed by a five-month prison sentence for income tax evasion, has denied Rose the honor he probably relishes more than any other—inclusion in baseball's Hall of Fame.

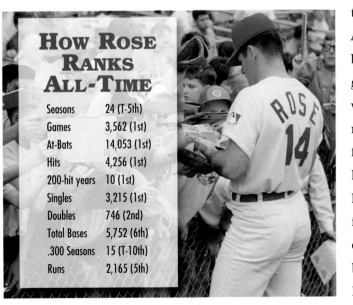

HOW ROSE RANKS ALL-TIME

Seasons	24 (T-5th)
Games	3,562 (1st)
At-Bats	14,053 (1st)
Hits	4,256 (1st)
200-hit years	10 (1st)
Singles	3,215 (1st)
Doubles	746 (2nd)
Total Bases	5,752 (6th)
.300 Seasons	15 (T-10th)
Runs	2,165 (5th)

> **Koufax is the greatest. He's the best pitcher I've ever seen.**
>
> JUAN MARICHAL, 1966

SANDY KOUFAX 28

P *1955-1966: DODGERS*

The ball shot out of his left hand and hurtled plateward in a white blur. The contorted grimace on Sandy Koufax's thin face was easier to see than the missile he had just launched. Such was the plight of overmatched National League hitters who had to face the Los Angeles Dodgers' ace during the most dominant six-year pitching exhibition of the second half-century.

Simply stated, the kid from Brooklyn was not your normal, everyday lefthander, from the day in 1955 when he joined his hometown Dodgers (skipping the minor leagues) until a day in 1966 when he told stunned Los Angeles fans he was retiring after 12 seasons because of an arthritic elbow he didn't want to damage beyond repair. The decision was shocking because Koufax, at age 30, had just completed a 27-9 season and a 129-47 six-year run that had vaulted him to the top of the pitching charts.

But that was typical Koufax, an intelligent, straight-shooting pragmatist who didn't mince words off the field or pitches on it. His 6-foot-2 frame held 210 pounds of muscle that delivered a blazing fastball and nasty curve to intimidated batters. When Koufax was "on," he left a trail of wins, strikeouts and no-hitters that cut a wide swath through baseball's record book.

Koufax, who was signed out of the University of Cincinnati, struggled with control and self-confidence through six mediocre seasons before transforming into a proficient pitching machine. From 1961-66, he was close to perfection. His .733 winning percentage was complemented by a record five consecutive N.L. ERA titles, one MVP, three Cy Young Awards, four strikeout titles and a 0.95 ERA and 4-3 record in three World Series—two that produced Dodger championships.

Koufax, who combined with Don Drysdale to form one of the best 1-2 pitching punches in history, twice fanned 18 batters in a game and struck out a then-record 382 in 1965, the same year he pitched a perfect game against Chicago— one of his four no-hitters. He retired with a 165-87 record.

ACE IN THE HOLE

Since 1950, only six pitchers have won 25 or more games during a season in which their team won the World Series. Koufax did it twice:

Year	Pitcher/Team	Record
1961	Whitey Ford, Yankees	25-4
1963	Sandy Koufax, Dodgers	25-5
1965	Sandy Koufax, Dodgers	26-8
1968	Denny McLain, Tigers	31-6
1969	Tom Seaver, Mets	25-7
1974	Catfish Hunter, A's	25-12
1978	Ron Guidry, Yankees	25-3

66 (Speaker) used to drive the opposition crazy (by playing so shallow). He had an unbelievable instinct. He could sense a ball that was going deep if he was in short center. You'd drive the ball deep and he was waiting for it. 99

CHUCK DRESSEN, 1956
FORMER PLAYER AND MANAGER

TRIS 29 SPEAKER

◆ OF ◆ *1907-1928: RED SOX, INDIANS, SENATORS, ATHLETICS*

He was easy to spot. The 6-foot, prematurely gray center fielder would position himself about 30 or 40 feet behind second base, ready to dart forward and cut off a potential hit or sprint back for anything over his head. Tris Speaker brazenly dared American League hitters to take their best shot, a challenge he answered emphatically with sure hands, lightning quickness, speed and a

powerful left arm that gave him status as the best defensive player in the game.

The irony is that Speaker seldom is remembered as one of baseball's greatest hitters, thanks primarily to his unfortunate career parallel with 12-time A.L. batting champion Ty Cobb. But over a 22-year career that began in 1907 with the Boston Red Sox, the "Gray Eagle" posted a .345 average, topping the .350 mark nine times, while managing only one batting crown (1916). He collected a major league-record 792 doubles, leading the A.L. eight times, and still ranks among all-time leaders in hits (3,514), triples (222) and runs (1,882).

Speaker stood deep in the box, holding his bat hip high, and attacked the ball from a closed, crouching lefthanded stance. He was a gap-finding, extra-base machine, thanks to outstanding speed that punished momentary

bobbles and helped him execute 432 steals. Only Cobb stood in the way of multiple batting titles.

Cobb, however, couldn't match Speaker's outfield cunning and nobody before or since has patrolled center field with such daring and aplomb. Believing that singles he could cut off would far outnumber triples that would sail over his head, Speaker played the shallowest center field in history, in effect serving as a fifth infielder. He loved to dart behind unsuspecting runners at second base for a pickoff and he twice tied the A.L. record with 35 assists.

Speaker was the centerpiece for three World Series champions, two with Boston (1912 and '15) and one (1920) during his eight-year run as player-manager at Cleveland. He was part of the great 1912 Boston outfield that included Duffy Lewis and Harry Hooper.

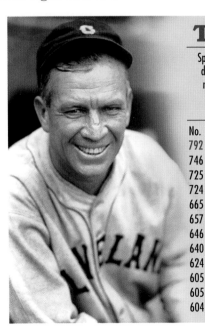

TWO-TIMING

Speaker holds the career record for doubles and shares the record for most times leading the league in that category. The numbers are through the 2005 season:

No.	Player	Led Lg.
792	Tris Speaker	8
746	Pete Rose	5
725	Stan Musial	8
724	Ty Cobb	3
665	George Brett	2
657	Nap Lajoie	5
646	Carl Yastrzemski	3
640	Honus Wagner	7
624	Hank Aaron	4
605	Paul Waner	2
605	Paul Molitor	2
604	Craig Biggio	3

MIKE 30 SCHMIDT

3B *1972-1989: PHILLIES*

Brooks Robinson and Pie Traynor had the golden gloves. Eddie Mathews and Harmon Killebrew had the game-breaking power. But no third baseman in the game's long history could match the near-perfect blend of defense, run production and speed that Mike Schmidt showcased during a Hall of Fame career in Philadelphia.

Over an 18-year run that opened in 1972, the even-tempered, always-cool Schmidt used those tools to help the Phillies carve out the most successful period in franchise history. He was the clubhouse leader and driving force for a team that won five National League East Division titles, two pennants and the 1980 World Series. In the process, he also carved out a personal legacy that put him in the select company of some of the game's greatest all-around players.

Every time the 6-foot-2 Schmidt walked to the plate, there was an air of expectancy. From his righthanded upright stance with bat held high and feet spread well apart he was a home run waiting to happen—a big swing with plenty of bat speed and power to all fields. Thirteen times he hit 30 or more home runs in a season and a record eight times he led or shared N.L. home hon-

ors en route to a career total of 548. From 1974 through 1987, which includes the strike-shortened 1981 campaign, he averaged 36.5 home runs and topped 100 RBIs nine times.

Schmidt, who played in 10 All-Star Games, also earned three MVP awards with home run-RBI combinations of 48-121 (1980), 37-119 (1986) and 31-91 (in a 102-game 1981 strike season). Sometimes lost in Schmidt's power numbers are his signature moments—a four-homer 1976 game at Chicago and a three-run, ninth-inning 1987 shot that gave the Phillies a dramatic win over Pittsburgh and Schmidt membership in baseball's elite "500 club."

But the number "10" is what really separates Schmidt from the other great power-hitting third basemen. That's how many Gold Gloves he won, second only to Robinson's 16.

FAST COMPANY

Schmidt, who won or shared an N.L.-record eight home run titles, ranks among baseball's all-time sluggers in 100-RBI and 30-homer seasons:

Player	100 RBI	30 HR	Total
Hank Aaron	11	15	26
Babe Ruth	13	13	26
Barry Bonds	12	14	26
Jimmie Foxx	13	12	25
Lou Gehrig	13	10	23
Mike Schmidt	9	13	22
Willie Mays	10	11	21
Sammy Sosa	9	11	20
Rafael Palmeiro	10	10	20
Manny Ramirez	10	10	20

"(Schmidt) gave us 110 percent every single night in every single at-bat. He set the standard for professionalism around here."

Bill Giles

Phillies Chairman
The Sporting News, 1990

66 Lajoie was one of the most
rugged hitters I ever faced.
He'd take your leg off with a
line drive, turn the third
baseman around like a
swinging door and powder the
hand of the left fielder. 99

CY YOUNG
THE SPORTING NEWS, 1950

NAPOLEON 31
LAJOIE

S tylish, graceful and handsome. Strong, intimidating and rugged. All of those seemingly contradictory descriptions applied to hard-hitting Napoleon Lajoie, a dark, bold-featured French-Canadian who left an indelible mark as one of the greatest and most important baseball stars of the 20th century's first decade.

Lajoie's historic contribution was made in 1901, his sixth major league season, when he jumped from the Philadelphia Phillies of the established National League to Connie Mack's Philadelphia Athletics of the new American League, giving the rival circuit its first superstar and instant credibility. Lajoie punctuated his controversial move by winning the century's first Triple Crown and posting a remarkable .422 average—still the highest single-season mark in A.L. history.

When the Phillies obtained an injunction prohibiting Lajoie from playing for the "other Philadelphia club" in 1902, Mack simply dealt his star to the A.L.'s franchise in Cleveland, where he remained until the final two seasons of his 21-year career—sitting out all games in Philadelphia. Cleveland fans formed a love affair with their big Frenchman, who reigned as the early century's premier offensive and defensive

second baseman.

The 6-foot-1, 200-pounder, easily recognized by his upturned collar and cap cocked stylishly to the side, glided effortlessly around the field, a graceful defender who led the A.L. in fielding percentage seven times. When Lajoie positioned himself deep in the box with his thick-handled bat, third basemen lived in fear of the vicious line drives he launched with a smooth, extended swing.

The oft-described "hardest hitter of the dead-ball era" backed up that reputation with a .339 career average, 3,252 hits, four 100-RBI seasons and three batting titles for generally weak Cleveland teams. But Lajoie is best remembered for the disputed 1910 title he lost by a fraction to Detroit rival Ty Cobb. A testimony to Lajoie's unwavering popularity was that the Indians were known as the "Naps" from 1905-09, years when he served as player/manager.

THE EXCLUSIVE .420 CLUB

Lajoie, in the American League's debut season, compiled an average that has been topped by only one hitter since 1900:

Year	Player	R	H	HR	RBI	Avg.
1924	Rogers Hornsby	121	227	25	94	.424
1901	Napoleon Lajoie	145	229	14	125	.422
1911	Ty Cobb	147	248	8	127	.420
1922	George Sisler	134	246	8	105	.420

STEVE 32 CARLTON

P 1965-1988: CARDINALS, PHILLIES, GIANTS, WHITE SOX, INDIANS, TWINS

His overpowering fastball and sweeping curve were good enough to humble most major league hitters. But they were only complementary pitches in the Hall of Fame arsenal of Steve Carlton. When "Lefty" unleashed his primary weapon with all the force his 6-foot-4, 210-pound frame could muster, the result was usually predictable and intimidating.

The Slider. Carlton went into his easy windup, right leg kicked forward and arm propelled the ball plateward from a three-quarters delivery. The batter, forced to think fastball, began his swing as the white blur moved ever closer. Suddenly, just before contact, the ball exploded—sideways and downward—as the batter realized his mistake, a split second too late.

The eccentric, intelligent Carlton, a martial arts practitioner whose outstanding conditioning and strength contributed to the force of his slider, was intensely focused and durable. He confounded hitters with his devastating pitches and pinpoint control over a 24-year career (1965-88) that produced 329 victories, four Cy Young Awards and 4,136 strikeouts—a total that ranks fourth all-time. Only once over a 17-season stretch (the strike-shortened 1981 campaign) did the 10-time All-Star selection work fewer than 229 innings.

Carlton, an intensely private man, resisted celebrity status and waged a war of silence against the media over the final decade-plus of his career. The six-time 20-game winner preferred the satisfaction he gained on the mound for Cardinals teams that won two National League pennants and one World Series in seven St. Louis seasons and Phillies teams that won five East Division titles, two pennants and one fall classic in 14-plus Philadelphia campaigns.

Carlton's signature season was 1972, his first in Philadelphia, when he finished 27-10 and led N.L. pitchers in ERA (1.97), strikeouts (310), complete games (30) and innings (346⅓) while pitching for a Phillies team that won only 59 games. But his best clutch performance came in the 1980 World Series when he defeated Kansas City twice and pitched the Game 6 clincher at Philadelphia.

A TALE OF TWO SEASONS

In Carlton's two best seasons, the Phillies posted contrasting records. There was nothing contrasting about his numbers in either Cy Young effort:

	1972	1980
Team	59-97	91-71
Carlton	27-10	24-9
IP	346.1	304.0
ERA	1.97	2.34
ER	76	79
BB	87	90
SO	310	286
WHIP	0.99	1.10

◆ SPORTING NEWS SELECTS BASEBALL'S 100 GREATEST PLAYERS ◆

66 Carlton is in a class by himself among lefthanders. If you don't get to Steve by the fifth inning, you might as well put your bats away. 99

BILL MADLOCK
FOUR-TIME BATTING CHAMPION
THE SPORTING NEWS, 1982

BOB 33 GIBSON

Bob Gibson's fastball was filled with the same intense rage as the man who launched it past helpless hitters for the better part of two decades. So was the sharp-breaking slider that some observers called the best of all time for a righthander. When Gibson was at his dazzling best, he almost made pitching seem unfair.

Look at it from the batter's point of view. Gibson, cap pulled down low over a glowering face, sets his powerful jaw and stares at his newest worst enemy. Everything about him looks mean as he begins a three-quarters delivery that will propel the ball homeward. The full-body follow-through is the killer. It begins with right leg extended sideways and ends with a full running step forward and toward the first base line. The man behind the scowl appears to be leaping toward you with hostile intent.

That intense, unfriendly style served Gibson well over the 17 seasons (1959-75) he anchored the St. Louis Cardinals' rotation, posting a 251-174 record. Teammates described a man with "pride, dedication and a must-win" demeanor on the mound; a man who would bury a fastball in the batter's rib when he wanted to make a point. But they described the off-field Gibson as eloquent, bright and fun-loving, although his barbs were delivered with a cutting edge.

Gibson, an outstanding fielder (nine Gold Gloves) and dangerous hitter (24 home runs), was a five-time 20-game winner and five-time All-Star Game performer. He is best remembered for a near-legendary 1968 season that produced a 22-9 record, 13 shutouts and a 1.12 ERA—the lowest ERA of the 20th century for a pitcher with 300 or more innings. He capped it with a National League MVP and Cy Young—the first of two he would win.

Gibson was an outstanding big-game pitcher. His 7-2 World Series record and 1.89 ERA anchored two Cardinal championships in three tries and featured a dominating 17-strikeout performance against Detroit in Game 1 of the 1968 classic.

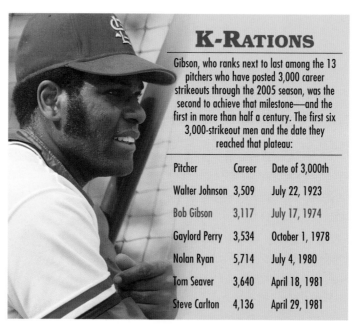

K-RATIONS

Gibson, who ranks next to last among the 13 pitchers who have posted 3,000 career strikeouts through the 2005 season, was the second to achieve that milestone—and the first in more than half a century. The first six 3,000-strikeout men and the date they reached that plateau:

Pitcher	Career	Date of 3,000th
Walter Johnson	3,509	July 22, 1923
Bob Gibson	3,117	July 17, 1974
Gaylord Perry	3,534	October 1, 1978
Nolan Ryan	5,714	July 4, 1980
Tom Seaver	3,640	April 18, 1981
Steve Carlton	4,136	April 29, 1981

"As long as I've been with him, I've never seen him smile on a day he's pitching. Whether he's winning or losing 1-0 or 12-0, he's all business."

RED SCHOENDIENST
THE SPORTING NEWS, 1972

TOM 34 SEAVER

P 1967-1986: METS, REDS, WHITE SOX, RED SOX

They billed him as the All-American boy and the image stayed with Tom Seaver throughout a successful 20-year career that started in New York and included stops at Cincinnati, Chicago and Boston. Articulate, handsome and intelligent off the field, Tom Terrific transformed into an intense, take-no-prisoners pitching machine when he climbed onto the mound.

Seaver charmed the tough New York market from his Rookie of the Year debut with the Mets in 1967 until he was sent to the Reds in an unpopular 1977 trade. His principle weapons were the hopping fastball, sharp-breaking curve and wicked slider he delivered with a powerful right arm and pinpoint control. But his secrets to success were the scientifically crafted delivery that saved his arm from wear and tear and the detailed book he kept on the strengths and weaknesses of every major league hitter.

Seaver literally exploded off the mound, driving hard toward the hitter with powerful legs and a well-muscled 210-pound body. He looked like a locomotive bursting from a tunnel. The delivery was compact and so low that Seaver's right leg literally dragged the ground during his follow-through. He could be an overpowering strikeout pitcher (19 in a 1970

game, more than 200 in nine consecutive seasons) one inning, a craftsman who set up hitters with off-speed pitches the next.

Seaver's signature performance in a career that produced 311 wins, five 20-victory seasons, 61 shutouts, 3,640 strikeouts and eight All-Star Game appearances came in 1969, when he finished 25-7 and anchored a staff that pitched Gil Hodges' Amazin' Mets to a shocking National League pennant and World Series win over powerful Baltimore. He was rewarded with the first of three Cy Young Awards.

Mets fans were shocked in 1977 when Seaver, midway through his 11th New York season, was traded to Cincinnati, where he completed a 21-6 effort. He never won 20 again, but he did post solid numbers en route to the 300-win plateau, which he reached with the White Sox in 1985.

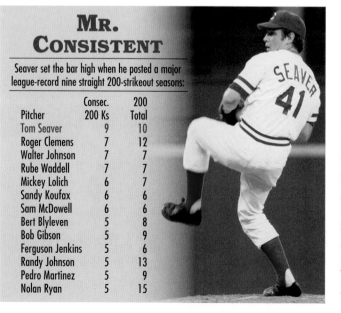

MR. CONSISTENT

Seaver set the bar high when he posted a major league-record nine straight 200-strikeout seasons:

Pitcher	Consec. 200 Ks	200 Total
Tom Seaver	9	10
Roger Clemens	7	12
Walter Johnson	7	7
Rube Waddell	7	7
Mickey Lolich	6	7
Sandy Koufax	6	6
Sam McDowell	6	6
Bert Blyleven	5	8
Bob Gibson	5	9
Ferguson Jenkins	5	6
Randy Johnson	5	13
Pedro Martinez	5	9
Nolan Ryan	5	15

> 66 I've never seen anyone so completely prepared, physically and mentally, so aware of himself in game situations. If not for his humanness, I don't think anybody would get any hits off him. 99

CARLTON FISK, 1985

GEORGE SISLER 35

1B *1915-1930: BROWNS, SENATORS, BRAVES*

H e was the quiet man in a league that showcased Ty Cobb and Babe Ruth and in a city that heaped its praise on St. Louis rival Rogers Hornsby. But the backseat George Sisler took to those colorful personalities was not reflected in his remarkable 15-year major league record, most of which he fashioned for the lowly St. Louis Browns.

The 170-pound Sisler, who was Hall of Fame contemporary Frank Frisch's "perfect player," brought manners and gentility to an era that was lacking in both. Modest and self-effacing, the University of Michigan graduate played with a quiet self-confidence that was not lost on opponents and fans. He emerged on the big-league scene in 1915 as a lefthanded pitcher and quickly made the transition to first base—a position he mastered with grace and superior quickness.

But Sisler's real magic could be found in the 42-ounce hickory bat he used like a wand to direct balls all over the park. The choke-hitting lefthander was a line-drive slasher who could muscle mistake pitches over the right field wall. Contemporaries were most impressed by the mechanical perfection from which he seldom wavered.

Sisler batted .353, .341 and .352 from 1917-19, but that was merely an appetizer. In a remarkable three-year exhibition from 1920-22, he posted averages of .407, .371 and .420 while collecting 719 hits and striking out only 60 times. The 257 hits Sisler recorded in 1920 stood as a major league record for 84 years, and

the 41-game hitting streak he compiled in 1922 stood as a modern record until 1941, when Joe DiMaggio hit in 56 straight. He also averaged 110 RBIs and 132 runs while leading the American League twice in stolen bases.

Sisler was forced to sit out the 1923 season with sinusitis, a disease that caused double vision. And although he played another seven years with the Browns and Boston Braves, he never hit with the same ferocious consistency. Sisler, who compiled a .340 career average with 2,812 hits, retired in 1930 without experiencing postseason play.

THE HIT MAN COMETH

From 1920-22, Sisler posted hit totals of 257, 216 and 246. No player has come close to matching that three-season barrage:

Total	Player	Years
719	George Sisler	1920-22
703	Rogers Hornsby	1920-22
693	Bill Terry	1929-31
684	Joe Medwick	1935-37
682	Ichiro Suzuki	2002-04
678	Lloyd Waner	1927-29
676	Chuck Klein	1930-32
668	Ty Cobb	1910-12
664	Kirby Puckett	1986-88
660	Paul Waner	1927-29

66 He was a professional with the bat in his hands. He never stopped thinking. He was a menace every time he stepped to the plate. In the field, he was the picture player, the acme of grace and fluency. 99

BRANCH RICKEY
THE SPORTING NEWS, 1953

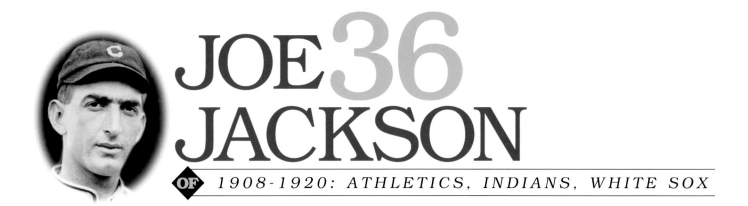

JOE 36 JACKSON

His name forever will be associated with the messiest episode in baseball history. His lifetime ban and exclusion from Hall of Fame consideration are viewed by many as a travesty of justice. But there's one thing nobody can take away from Shoeless Joe Jackson: his reputation as the greatest natural hitter in the game's long history.

Ty Cobb thought he was. An impressed Babe Ruth copied his batting style. Other contemporaries, such as Tris Speaker, Nap Lajoie and Eddie Collins, marveled at the slashing line drives that whipped off his oversized bat during the 13 years (1908-20) he starred for the Philadelphia Athletics, Cleveland Indians and Chicago White Sox.

The lefthanded-hitting, righthanded-throwing left fielder never met a pitcher he couldn't hit. Jackson stood well back in the box, feet close together, and unleashed his big, even swing— unlike the short, punching jabs of other top dead-ball hitters. The only thing missing from the 6-1, 200-pounder's offensive arsenal was the great speed that gave Cobb the additional hits he needed to win 12 batting championships. Jackson, who topped the 200-hit plateau four times, batted .408 for the Indians in 1911—losing the bat-ting title to Cobb's .420—and .395 the following year en route to a whopping .356 career mark, third all-time behind Cobb and Rogers Hornsby.

Jackson, who earned his nickname as a minor leaguer when he played a game in his stocking feet because of a blister, helped the White Sox to a championship in 1917. But his exact role in the 1919 Black Sox scandal will never be known. There's no doubt the illiterate country kid from the Carolina hill country, perhaps caught up unwittingly in something he did not fully understand, enjoyed an outstanding World Series against Cincinnati (.375, a record 12 hits, no errors) while teammates were helping the Reds to victory. One of eight White Sox players banned for life by then-commissioner Kenesaw Mountain Landis, Jackson never played another big-league game—a punishment, right or wrong, that continued long after his 1951 death.

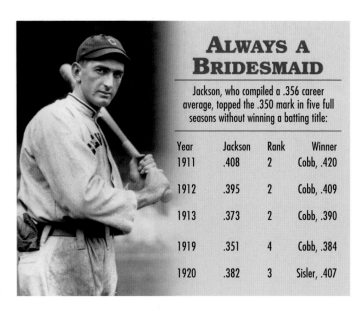

ALWAYS A BRIDESMAID

Jackson, who compiled a .356 career average, topped the .350 mark in five full seasons without winning a batting title:

Year	Jackson	Rank	Winner
1911	.408	2	Cobb, .420
1912	.395	2	Cobb, .409
1913	.373	2	Cobb, .390
1919	.351	4	Cobb, .384
1920	.382	3	Sisler, .407

> 66 I copied Jackson's batting style because I thought he was the greatest hitter I had ever seen. I still think the same. 99

BABE RUTH, 1942

BOB 37 FELLER

P *1936-1941, 1945-1956: INDIANS*

He whirled into major league prominence in 1936 as a naive 17-year-old farmboy and retired two decades later as one of the most sophisticated strikeout machines in baseball history. Through most of his 18 seasons with the Cleveland Indians, Bob Feller must have seemed like a white blur to hitters trying to catch up with his 98-plus mph fastballs.

Feller, a 6-foot, high-kicking righthander who never played a minor league game, stepped off the Van Meter, Iowa, farm and struck out 15 St. Louis Browns in his first big-league start. Three weeks later, he tied Dizzy Dean's major league record with 17 strikeouts in a two-hit win over the Philadelpha Athletics. When his short rookie season ended, Feller returned home and finished high school.

Feller's pitching ledger is filled with strikeouts (2,581), no-hitters (3), one-hitters (12) and 20-win seasons (6). But those numbers and his 266-162 career record could have been a lot higher if not for the three-plus seasons he spent winning battle stars for the Navy during World War II. Baseball's All-American boy, who could have avoided military duty because his father was dying of cancer, chose instead to serve his country at age 23—after

three straight 20-win seasons.

That was typical Feller, who once insisted on taking a pay cut after what he considered a bad season. He was proud, outspoken, opinionated and self-promoting—but the strutting arrogance he displayed on the mound did not draw criticism from the hitters he dominated. Feller's premier season was 1940, when, at age 21, he pitched an opening-day no-hitter and went on to compile a 27-11 record with a 2.61 ERA and 261 strikeouts. He was 26-15 in 1946 with a career-high 348 strikeouts and career-low 2.18 ERA.

The biggest void in Feller's career was his inability to record a postseason victory. The five-time All-Star Game performer was 0-2 in Cleveland's 1948 World Series win and, surprisingly, he did not pitch as the Indians were swept in the 1954 fall classic by the New York Giants.

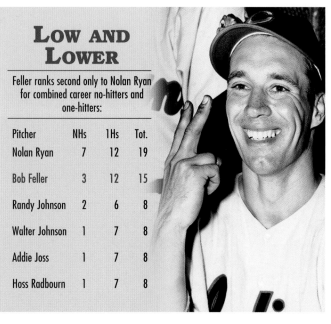

LOW AND LOWER

Feller ranks second only to Nolan Ryan for combined career no-hitters and one-hitters:

Pitcher	NHs	1Hs	Tot.
Nolan Ryan	7	12	19
Bob Feller	3	12	15
Randy Johnson	2	6	8
Walter Johnson	1	7	8
Addie Joss	1	7	8
Hoss Radbourn	1	7	8

" (Walter) Johnson was tops.
Feller isn't too far away. "

CY YOUNG, 1951

HANK 38 GREENBERG

1B *1930-1941, 1945-1947: TIGERS, PIRATES*

He was a self-made superstar, the big, clumsy New York City kid who transformed his ugly-duckling awkwardness into Hall of Fame grace. What Hank Greenberg lacked in natural talent he more than made up for with unyielding desire, hard work and intense dedication to his craft. Big Hank was an overachiever, a 6-foot-4 pounder who earned baseball success through mind-over-matter determination.

Nothing came easy for Greenberg, who made his major league debut for the Detroit Tigers in 1930 as a stumbling first baseman. He wasn't fast, a shortcoming he never could overcome, but he worked hard to improve his quickness, spent hours mastering defensive fundamentals and learned to hit the curveball in early morning sessions with weary batting practice pitchers. American League pitchers felt the crunch of Hank's gritty perseverance.

His 215-pound body cut a menacing figure and his big arms and roundhouse swing pounded the ball with Ruthian-like frequency, power and run production. Six times he topped 30 home runs, including a 58-homer 1938 season that left him only two short of Babe Ruth's single-season record, and four times he topped 145 RBIs,

including a 183-RBI 1937 season that left him eight short of Hack Wilson's record. Greenberg, a member of two Detroit championship teams, earned two A.L. MVP awards (1935 and '40) and his .313 career average defied the conventional profile of a power hitter.

The outspoken, articulate Greenberg, who later put those qualities to use as a front-office executive, finished his career with 331 home runs—a figure that would have been considerably higher if he had not lost four-plus seasons to World War II and another to a broken wrist, giving him a real career of less than 10 years. His defining moment came in 1945, when he hit a dramatic final-day grand slam to clinch the A.L. pennant for the Tigers and complete his first half season back from military duty. He added two more homers in a World Series victory over Chicago.

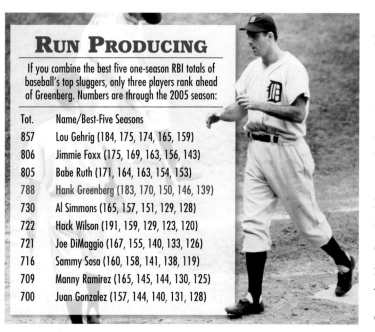

RUN PRODUCING

If you combine the best five one-season RBI totals of baseball's top sluggers, only three players rank ahead of Greenberg. Numbers are through the 2005 season:

Tot.	Name/Best-Five Seasons
857	Lou Gehrig (184, 175, 174, 165, 159)
806	Jimmie Foxx (175, 169, 163, 156, 143)
805	Babe Ruth (171, 164, 163, 154, 153)
788	Hank Greenberg (183, 170, 150, 146, 139)
730	Al Simmons (165, 157, 151, 129, 128)
722	Hack Wilson (191, 159, 129, 123, 120)
721	Joe DiMaggio (167, 155, 140, 133, 126)
716	Sammy Sosa (160, 158, 141, 138, 119)
709	Manny Ramirez (165, 145, 144, 130, 125)
700	Juan Gonzalez (157, 144, 140, 131, 128)

◆ SPORTING NEWS SELECTS BASEBALL'S 100 GREATEST PLAYERS ◆

> ❝Greenberg positively made a great hitter out of himself. He did it by constant practice. He'd come out to the park as early as 8 o'clock in the morning and hit for hours. He'd stay after games and hit until darkness made him quit.❞
>
> PAUL RICHARDS, 1953
> LONGTIME MANAGER AND EXECUTIVE

ERNIE 39 BANKS

His smile lit up Wrigley Field and his quick bat lit up National League scoreboards. Everything about Ernie Banks was contagious, from the boundless enthusiasm he brought to long-suffering Chicago fans to the grace and flair with which he roamed his shortstop and first base positions for 19 major league seasons. Never has an athletic love affair been consummated with more devotion than the one between Mr. Cub and Chicago's North Side fans.

The painfully shy Banks, who was plucked off the roster of the Negro League's Kansas City Monarchs in 1953, injected much-needed hope into a depressed franchise. His movement was quick and agile, his reflexes were magnificent, his eyesight was an exceptional 20/13 and his skinny 6-1, 180-pound frame packed a wallop that would inspire a new legion of "little man" power hitters. The secret was in his wrists and forearms, leading Hall of Fame pitcher Robin Roberts to marvel: "From the elbows down, he's got the muscles of a 230-pounder."

Banks also used a 31-ounce bat, proving that bat speed, not size, unlocked the secret to power-hitting success. He stood deep in the box, left foot crowding the plate, and stared blankly at the pitcher, fingers drumming rhythmically on the bat handle. Banks didn't swing at the ball; he lashed at it—with a deadly force that yielded spectacular results. Five times he topped 40 home runs en route to a career total of 512. He topped 100 RBIs eight times, played in 13 All-Star Games and captured consecutive MVPs (1958 and '59) with combined two-year totals of 92 home runs and 272 RBIs.

But nothing captures the essence of Banks better than the "let's play two" enthusiasm he always brought to the park, win or lose. He was one of the game's top goodwill ambassadors, a fan favorite who remained upbeat and happy while playing for Cubs teams that seldom posted winning records and never gave him a postseason opportunity that might have added luster to his outstanding career.

STAYING HOME

Banks is one of 11 players to hit more than 500 home runs with one team:

Player/Team	HRs
Hank Aaron, Braves	733
Babe Ruth, Yankees	659
Willie Mays, Giants	646
Harmon Killebrew, Twins	559
Mike Schmidt, Phillies	548
Sammy Sosa, Cubs	545
Mickey Mantle, Yankees	536
Barry Bonds, Giants	532
Ted Williams, Red Sox	521
Ernie Banks, Cubs	512
Met Ott, Giants	511

"Do you know of a better way to earn a living than playing baseball? Baseball isn't work to me. It's a game. Everything in baseball is fun for me."

ERNIE BANKS, 1961

YOGI 40 BERRA

◆ C ◆ 1946-1963, 1965: YANKEES, METS

The squat, gnome-like body, topped by a face locked in permanent caricature, inspired jokes and friendly barbs. But there was nothing funny about the surprising agility, fast feet and slashing bat that carried Yogi Berra to Hall of Fame heights as the backstop for one of the greatest dynasties in sports history. The lovable, gregarious personality defines Berra the man, but the 14 World Series in which he showcased his talents for the New York Yankees define his baseball legacy.

It was easy to dismiss the 5-foot-8, 190-pound, barrel-chested Berra when he slipped into his baggy No. 8 Yankees uniform for the first time in 1946. But teammates and fans quickly learned to appreciate the boyish enthusiasm with which the knock-kneed youngster moved behind the plate and the desire with which he enhanced his catching skills under the tutelage of fading star Bill Dickey. His quickness was deceptive, his arm was strong if occasionally erratic.

But the bat is what separated Yogi from other big-league catchers. A lefthanded hitter, he stood at the plate with a nervous air of expectancy and used his quick wrists to slash pitches with power to all fields. Berra, a notorious bad-ball hitter who seldom struck out, was tough to pitch to and especially dangerous with the game on the line. Three A.L. MVP awards (1951, 1954, 1955) offer testimony to the respect he earned over a 19-year career that ended in 1965.

Berra is best known for the charming malaprops he delivered with gravelly voiced innocence and endearing honesty, enhancing his image as "the guy next door." But he had a clever baseball mind that enabled him to masterfully handle pitchers, both as a player and later a pennant-winning manager for the Yankees and New York Mets.

Berra played for an incredible 10 World Series champions and retired with fall classic records for games (75), at-bats (259) and hits (71) and top-five rankings with 39 RBIs (second) and 12 home runs (third). He also played in 15 All-Star Games.

MR. WORLD SERIES

How Berra ranks in the World Series record book (through 2004):

Series won	10 (1st)
Games	75 (1st)
At-bats	259 (1st)
Runs	41 (2nd)
Hits	71 (1st)
Singles	49 (1st)
Doubles	10 (T-1st)
Home runs	12 (3rd)
Total bases	117 (2nd)
RBIs	39 (2nd)
Walks	32 (3rd)

“Mr. Berra was second only to Joe DiMaggio in all-around ability among the players I managed.”

CASEY STENGEL
THE SPORTING NEWS, 1971

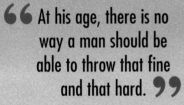

" At his age, there is no way a man should be able to throw that fine and that hard. **"**

WALT WEISS

MAJOR LEAGUE SHORTSTOP
THE SPORTING NEWS, 1990

NOLAN RYAN 41

P *1966-1993: METS, ANGELS, ASTROS, RANGERS*

The Nolan Ryan fastball made its first appearance on the radar gun in 1966 and was still being tracked in 1993, an amazing 27 years later. There was nothing subtle about it. At Ryan's peak, it shot to the plate at more than 100 mph. In Ryan's final season, it reached only 95—the man's one concession to age. The pitching legacy it helped produce might withstand the test of time.

Start with the strikeouts—5,714 of them, 1,212 more than second-place Roger Clemens. Then the no-hitters—seven, three more than second-place Sandy Koufax. Then the innings (5,386), victories (324), shutouts (61), one-hitters (12) and countless longevity records Ryan piled up over a career that started with the New York Mets and included long stints with the California Angels, Houston Astros and Texas Rangers.

Simply stated, Ryan was master of the attention-getting performance—a no-hitter or strikeout record waiting to happen. But unlike the great Walter Johnson, the 6-foot-2 Ryan was not a one-pitch wonder. Wild and erratic in the early years, Ryan's steady improvement drew direct parallel to his mastery of a nasty curveball that froze fastball-thinking hitters and a changeup that almost seemed unfair.

That was the perception among American League hitters in 1973 and '74 when the big righthander posted consecutive 21-16 and 22-16 records, set a single-season strikeout mark with 383, pitched three no-hitters and

recorded impressive hits-per-inning marks for sub-.500 Angels teams. Ryan never again won 20 games and he never won a Cy Young, but an insatiable work ethic and commitment to conditioning painted an aura of invincibility around his bionic arm.

Once criticized as a .500 pitcher, Ryan's greatest popularity came in the 1990s when he continued to dominate batters, recorded his 300th win and added no-hitters Nos. 6 and 7—for the Rangers at ages 43 and 44. Ryan, who pitched in five All-Star Games, spent most of his years with weak teams as his 292 losses suggest, but he did pitch for the Amazin' Mets in their 1969 World Series victory over Baltimore.

GOLDEN OLDIES

Ryan is one of four pitchers to throw no-hitters after their 40th birthday—the only one to do it twice:

Pitcher	Team	Date	Age
Nolan Ryan	Rangers	5-1-91	44 (3 months)
Nolan Ryan	Rangers	6-11-90	43 (4 months)
Cy Young	Red Sox	6-30-08	41 (3 months)
Randy Johnson	D-backs	5-18-2004	40 (8 months)
Warren Spahn	Braves	4-28-61	40 (0 months)

MEL 42 OTT

◆OF◆ *1926-1947: GIANTS*

He was a living, breathing oxymoron, a diminutive 5-foot-9, 170-pound boy wonder who dared to challenge Babe Ruth for home run-hitting superiority in New York City. When Mel Ott lifted his famous right leg and lashed into another pitch, Giants fans stationed in the Polo Grounds' short right field bleachers braced—a ritual they practiced enthusiastically for 22 seasons.

A 16-year-old Ott and his impressive lefthanded swing showed up on the Giants' doorstep in 1925 and spent a season learning the game at the side of manager John McGraw. At age 17 he played his first big-league game, at 19 he belted 18 home runs and at 20 he vaulted into prominence with a 42-homer, 151-RBI season—the first of eight 30-homer efforts that would define Ott's career.

Ottie, always smiling and personable, won over fans with his defensive hustle and cat-like quickness in right field, where he expertly played caroms off the oddly shaped wall. But most of all they loved his distinctive batting style. A .304 career hitter, he crowded the plate with feet apart and raised his right leg, about knee high, as the pitcher began his delivery. In one instantaneous motion, the bat

pulled back, the foot planted and he swung.

Ott, a dead-pull hitter who seldom struck out, was tailor-made for the longball-friendly Polo Grounds (257 feet down the right field line), where he drilled 325 of his 511 career home runs. In an incredible 18-year stretch from 1928 through 1945, he led the Giants in homers every year, never falling below 18. He was the National League leader in six of those years and he topped 100 RBIs nine times as the primary run-producer for a team built around defense and pitching.

By the time Ott became the N.L.'s first 500-homer man in 1945, he also was serving as player/manager of the Giants, a role he filled for six seasons. Ott, who played in 11 All-Star Games, contributed to three New York pennant-winners, but only one World Series champion (1933).

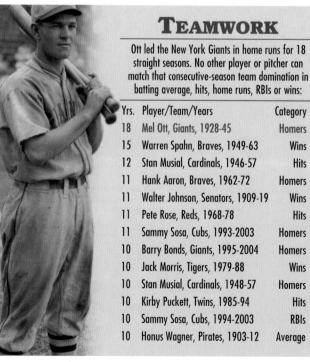

TEAMWORK

Ott led the New York Giants in home runs for 18 straight seasons. No other player or pitcher can match that consecutive-season team domination in batting average, hits, home runs, RBIs or wins:

Yrs.	Player/Team/Years	Category
18	Mel Ott, Giants, 1928-45	Homers
15	Warren Spahn, Braves, 1949-63	Wins
12	Stan Musial, Cardinals, 1946-57	Hits
11	Hank Aaron, Braves, 1962-72	Homers
11	Walter Johnson, Senators, 1909-19	Wins
11	Pete Rose, Reds, 1968-78	Hits
11	Sammy Sosa, Cubs, 1993-2003	Homers
10	Barry Bonds, Giants, 1995-2004	Homers
10	Jack Morris, Tigers, 1979-88	Wins
10	Stan Musial, Cardinals, 1948-57	Homers
10	Kirby Puckett, Twins, 1985-94	Hits
10	Sammy Sosa, Cubs, 1994-2003	RBIs
10	Honus Wagner, Pirates, 1903-12	Average

◆ SPORTING NEWS SELECTS BASEBALL'S 100 GREATEST PLAYERS ◆

> ❝ (Simmons) was great all-around, running, fielding and throwing as well as hitting and as a competitor. There never was a greater left fielder in going to the line and holding a double to a single. ❞
>
> JOE CRONIN
> THE SPORTING NEWS, 1971

AL 43 SIMMONS

A haughty swagger and defiance complemented his driving-force status for one of the greatest teams ever assembled. The vicious line drives Al Simmons slashed out for 20 big-league seasons emulated the ones stroked by his boyhood hero, Ty Cobb. Some Simmons watchers called him the second-best righthanded hitter behind Rogers Hornsby; others classified him as the second-best all-around player of his era behind Cobb himself.

Simmons' .334 career average, which included 2,927 hits and 307 home runs, says a lot. But it doesn't capture the quiet confidence with which he ran the bases, played left field and gunned down aggressive runners with a shotgun arm. He seldom made a mistake, a quality not lost on Philadelphia manager Connie Mack, who made him the centerpiece of his 1929, '30 and '31 pennant-winning Athletics—a star-studded team that captured two straight World Series.

Simmons' righthanded batting style was not the stuff of which instructional films are made. He stood deep in the box, feet close together, and took a long stride toward third base—as if bailing out. But "Bucketfoot Al" had the uncanny ability to keep his hips and weight in control, a discipline that allowed him

to hit to the opposite field with unusual power. Two A.L. batting titles (.381 and .390) and 12 100-RBI seasons cemented Simmons' status as one of the great hitters of his time.

So did the three-year crush he delivered on A.L. pitchers during the A's pennant seasons. He batted .378 over those three years and averaged 208 hits, 124 runs, 31 homers and 150 RBIs. He added six home runs and 17 RBIs in the three World Series.

But some of the luster was lost when Mack, strapped financially by the Great Depression, sold Simmons' contract after the 1932 season, sentencing his veteran star to wander from team to team over the next decade. Simmons served as a hired gun for seven different teams, always hitting but never regaining the top form of his early years with the A's.

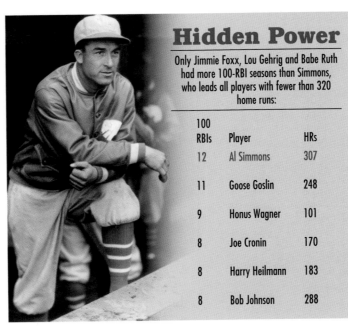

Hidden Power

Only Jimmie Foxx, Lou Gehrig and Babe Ruth had more 100-RBI seasons than Simmons, who leads all players with fewer than 320 home runs:

100 RBIs	Player	HRs
12	Al Simmons	307
11	Goose Goslin	248
9	Honus Wagner	101
8	Joe Cronin	170
8	Harry Heilmann	183
8	Bob Johnson	288

JACKIE ROBINSON 44

2B *1947-1956: DODGERS*

Jackie Robinson will be remembered as a pioneer, the man who broke baseball's color barrier for Branch Rickey's Brooklyn Dodgers in 1947 and ushered in a second half-century of hope and opportunity. But sometimes lost in the shadow of Robinson's overwhelming achievement is the marvelous athletic ability that would have been enough to get him Hall of Fame recognition in a normal, integrated baseball society.

Any assessment of Robinson's career has to be made in the context of what he endured on the field—racial epithets, name-calling, threats, spikings and other cruel admonitions. Always, as demanded by Rickey, he bit his lip and turned the other cheek, letting his hitting, baserunning and fielding reap the only revenge he would be allowed. To say that Robinson, a four-sport athlete at UCLA, performed admirably under pressure is something of an understatement.

As a hitter, the 5-foot-11 righthander was always dangerous and unpredictable, whether using his great speed to beat out a bunt, driving a ball into the gap or hitting behind a runner with uncanny precision. As a baserunner, he was aggressive and smart, a dancing bandit who distracted pitchers, rattled defenses and ignited the Dodgers' attack. As a second baseman, he was smooth, graceful and sure-handed, a pressure performer who made big plays in key situations.

It's no coincidence the Dodgers captured six pennants and their only Brooklyn World Series with Robinson providing the offensive spark. As a 28-year-old rookie playing under an intense spotlight, he batted .297. Two years later, he led N.L. hitters with a .342 average and drove in 124 runs. He scored 100 runs six times and his 197 career stolen bases included 19 steals of home.

But more than anything else, Robinson brought to the game a fierce pride and competitive spirit that allowed him to fight through adversity and win the respect of both teammates and opponents. That respect was manifested in his 1947 Rookie of the Year award, 1949 N.L. MVP and the six All-Star Games in which he played.

AN ARTFUL DODGER

Harassed, cursed and distracted through most of his 10 major league seasons, Robinson still posted outstanding numbers for Dodgers teams that won six N.L. pennants and one World Series:

Average	.311
Hits	1,518
Runs	947
Doubles	273
Triples	54
Stolen bases	197
World Series games	38
World Series hits	32
World Series runs	22

♦ SPORTING NEWS SELECTS BASEBALL'S 100 GREATEST PLAYERS ♦

"He was a great competitor who could do it all. He was a great player, a manager's dream. ...If I had to go to war, I'd want him on my side."

LEO DUROCHER, 1972

CARL 45 HUBBELL

Early century hitters called it the "fadeaway." Batters in the 1920s and '30s labeled it the "butterfly" or "reverse curve." By any name and by all accounts, the two kinds of screwballs Carl Hubbell delivered to National League hitters with uncanny accuracy from 1928-43 were downright nasty—and borderline unhittable.

Amazingly, the tall, Lincolnesque lefthander did not deliver his first screwgie to a major leaguer until age 25, thanks to the perception among coaches and managers that the pitch required an unnatural twisting motion that would destroy his arm. But Hubbell, who was blessed with exceptionally long and flexible wrists, refused to give in to cynics and rode his so-called "gimmick pitch" all the way to the Hall of Fame.

The high-kicking, fast-working Hubbell, the "Meal Ticket" for a New York Giants staff that produced three pennants and one World Series championship, undressed most of the game's top hitters with a sidearm screwball that faded down and away from righthanders and an overhand screwball that came in straight before suddenly dropping into oblivion. King Carl was especially tough on righthanders and his outstanding control allowed him to throw the pitch on any count.

The mild-mannered Hubbell, son of an Oklahoma pecan farmer, fashioned an impressive five-year run (1933-37) in which he was 115-50 and earned two MVP awards. In 1933, he posted a 23-12 record and 1.66 ERA before winning twice in a World Series victory over Washington. In 1936, he was 26-6 with a 2.31 ERA before splitting two decisions in a World Series loss to the New York Yankees.

Hubbell also recorded three of baseball's most memorable feats—an 18-inning 1-0 victory over the Cardinals in 1933; consecutive strikeouts of Babe Ruth, Lou Gehrig, Jimmie Foxx, Al Simmons and Joe Cronin in the 1934 All-Star Game; and a major league-record 24 straight wins in 1936-37. Hubbell, who worked in five All-Star Games, finally succumbed to the long-predicted arm trouble in 1943, but not before carving out 253 wins and a sparkling .622 career winning percentage.

GIANT STEPS

Hubbell is one of seven 20th-century pitchers to compile at least 250 wins with a .600 winning percentage, a below-3.00 ERA and 3,500 innings (totals through the 2005 season):

Pitcher	W	L	Pct.	ERA	IP
Cy Young	511	316	.618	2.63	7,356
Christy Mathewson	373	188	.665	2.13	4,780.2
Grover Alexander	373	208	.642	2.56	5,190
Eddie Plank	326	194	.627	2.35	4,495.2
Tom Seaver	311	205	.603	2.86	4,782.2
Jim Palmer	268	152	.638	2.86	3,948
Carl Hubbell	253	154	.622	2.98	3,590.1

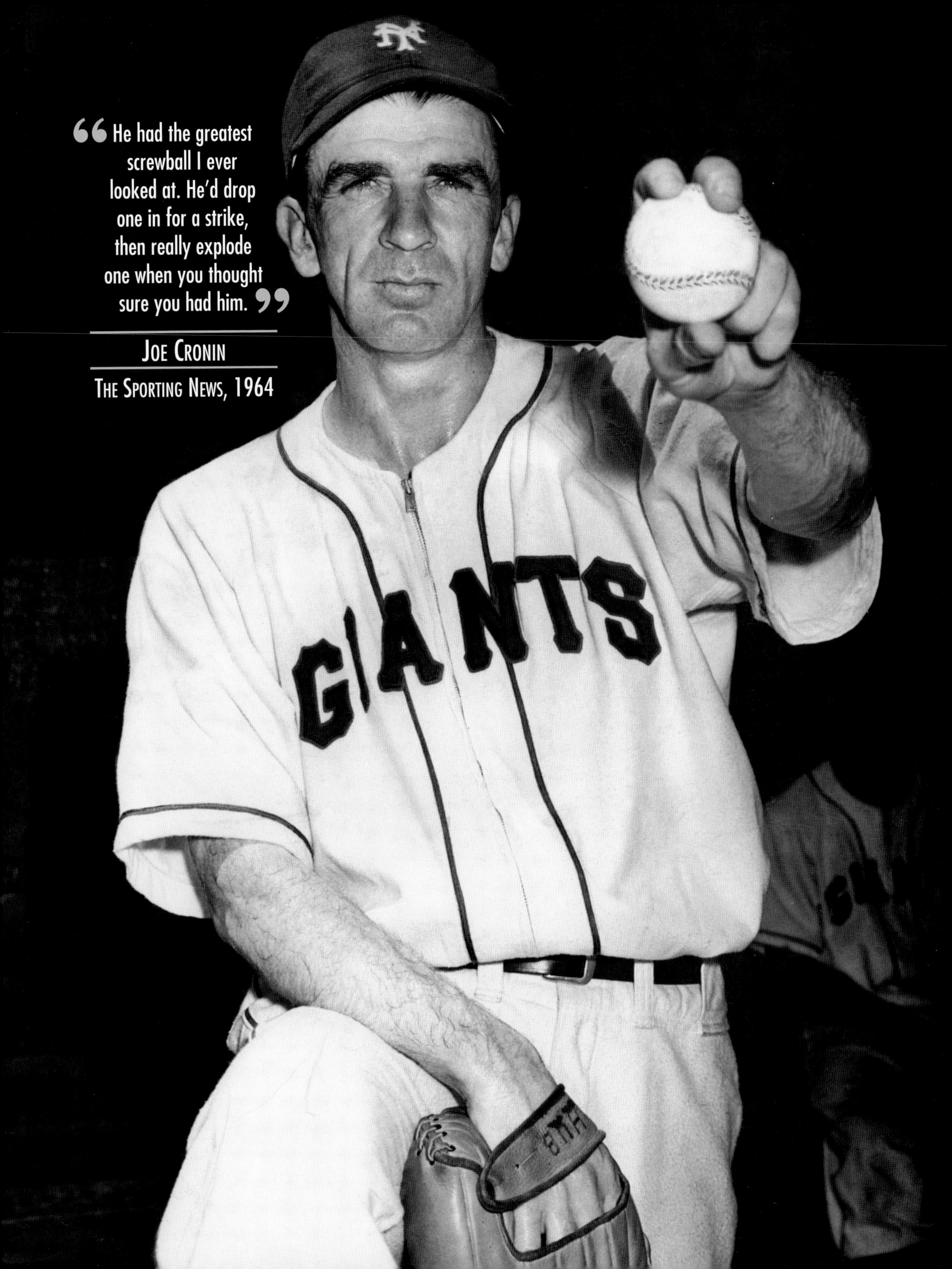

> “He had the greatest screwball I ever looked at. He’d drop one in for a strike, then really explode one when you thought sure you had him.”

Joe Cronin

The Sporting News, 1964

> " (Gehringer) was always No. 1 (second baseman) in my book. Charley made every play and he made it effortlessly. "

JOE DIMAGGIO, 1963

CHARLEY 46 GEHRINGER

2B *1924-1942: TIGERS*

They called him The Mechanical Man. And indeed Charley Gehringer did everything with machine-like precision—an effortless, graceful consistency that belied the competitive spirit raging within. He was always stylish, polished and quiet, prompting former teammate Mickey Cochrane to observe, "He says hello on opening day, goodbye closing day and, in between, hits .350."

All of Gehringer's in-betweens came for Detroit, where he honed his picture-book batting style under the tutelage of manager Ty Cobb from 1924-26 and began his 19-year run as one of the smoothest second basemen the game has produced. The sad-faced former Michigan farmboy made everything look easy with his classy glove, whether ranging to his left, charging rollers or retreating to the outfield for short fly balls. What the seven-time A.L. fielding percentage leader lacked in showmanship he more than made up for with a sleep-inducing consistency that fit his expressionless demeanor.

At the plate, the lefthanded-hitting Gehringer stood erect and motionless, a cat preparing to pounce. Ever patient, he worked the pitcher hard and drove the ball to all fields with extra-base power.

The 6-foot Gehringer, one of the best two-strike hitters of his era, topped the .300 mark 13 times en route to a career .320 average and won an A.L. batting title (.371) and MVP award in 1937.

Gehringer could play the role of instigator (he topped 100 runs scored 12 times) or run-producer (seven 100-RBI seasons) while raining out hits with amazing consistency. In 1929 he led the A.L. in runs (131), hits (215), doubles (45) and triples (19) and he reached the magic 200-hit plateau five straight years and seven times in a nine-season stretch.

Gehringer, who played in the first six All-Star Games, was a middle-infield anchor for powerful Detroit teams that won 1934, '35 and '40 pennants and the 1935 World Series. Not surprisingly, Gehringer was a .321 hitter in fall classic play.

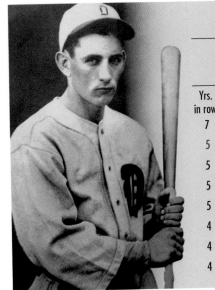

HITTING STRIDE

Through 2005, Gehringer was one of five players since 1900 to post 200 or more hits in five consecutive seasons:

Yrs. in row	Name	Seasons	Total	Avg.
7	Wade Boggs	1983-89	1,479	211.3
5	Charley Gehringer	1933-37	1,055	211
5	Chuck Klein	1929-33	1,118	223.6
5	Al Simmons	1929-33	1,039	207.8
5	Ichiro Suzuki	2001-05	1,130	226
4	Kirby Puckett	1986-89	879	219.8
4	Bill Terry	1929-32	918	229.5
4	Paul Waner	1927-30	877	219.3

BUCK 47
LEONARD

As one-half of the greatest 1-2 hitting punch in Negro League history, Buck Leonard made an indelible impression on a baseball community he would never be allowed to inhabit. "He was major league all the way," said Hall of Fame catcher Roy Campanella. And nobody who saw him play—black or white—would argue the point.

Unfortunately, Leonard's only contact with major league players would be in offseason barnstorming exhibitions that filled out the exhaustive year-round schedule of the pre-World War II black player. For 23 years, he competed in as many as three games per day and for 17 of those seasons he handled first base duty for the Homestead Grays, a Pittsburgh-based power that also featured catcher Josh Gibson, pitcher Satchel Paige and several other black stars.

The combination of Gibson, the Babe Ruth of the Negro Leagues, and Leonard, the so-called Lou Gehrig of the Negro Leagues, was offensive mayhem. Gibson, renowned for his long home runs, batted third; Leonard, who hit his homers frequently if not as far, batted fourth. Pitchers who worked around Gibson had to deal with a lefthanded batter who uncoiled into their fastballs from a

menacing crouch. He was a dead-pull hitter who produced runs and posted averages in the high .300s.

At 5-foot-10, 185 pounds, the stocky left-hander was not the prototypical first baseman. But nobody in any league could match Leonard's agility, powerful arm and ability to dig throws out of the dirt. Some observers called him quietly elegant. Others said his defense alone was worth the price of admission. His play around the bag mirrored his personality—steady, quiet and always dependable.

When baseball's color barrier fell in 1947, Leonard was 39 years old and past his prime, a self admission that reflected his unwillingness to pit diminishing talents against younger major leaguers. He was forced to settle for Hall of Fame recognition, which came in 1972 at age 64.

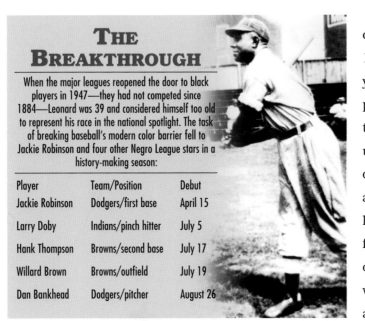

THE BREAKTHROUGH

When the major leagues reopened the door to black players in 1947—they had not competed since 1884—Leonard was 39 and considered himself too old to represent his race in the national spotlight. The task of breaking baseball's modern color barrier fell to Jackie Robinson and four other Negro League stars in a history-making season:

Player	Team/Position	Debut
Jackie Robinson	Dodgers/first base	April 15
Larry Doby	Indians/pinch hitter	July 5
Hank Thompson	Browns/second base	July 17
Willard Brown	Browns/outfield	July 19
Dan Bankhead	Dodgers/pitcher	August 26

"I love competition. It motivates me, stimulates me, excites me. I just love to hit the baseball in a big game."

REGGIE JACKSON

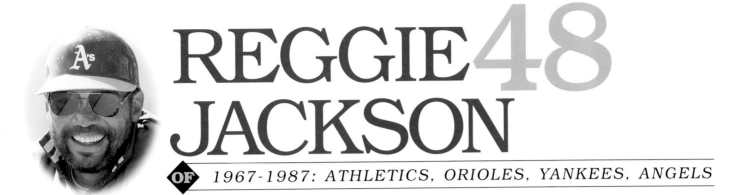

REGGIE 48
JACKSON

H e was charming and belligerent; cocky and self-effacing; articulate and crude; enigmatic and straightforward. You didn't just watch Reggie Jackson, you experienced him. The love-hate bond that fans, players and owners formed with the complex, often-contradictory kid from Wyncote, Pa., lasted 21 years, surviving 563 home runs and at least that many well-publicized tantrums.

Jackson, muscular and with an all-or-nothing corkscrew lefthanded swing, enjoyed several baseball lives. He was the heart and soul of an Oakland team that won three straight World Series (1972, '73 and '74); the straw that stirred a Yankees team that won two straight Series (1977 and '78); and "Mr. October," who rose to his greatest heights in the 11 League Championship Series and five World Series in which he hit 17 home runs for the A's, Yankees and California Angels.

The bottom line on Jackson was drama—and emotion, which he kept upfront for all the paying customers to see. A Jackson home run was majestic and he exulted accordingly, with a slow, measured trot. Jackson strikeouts (all 2,597 of them) were exciting and he fumed with demonstrative vigor. Jackson's right field defense was erratic, his baserunning was daring but careless and his battles with owners, man-

agers, teammates and even himself were legendary.

But there's no denying the charisma, which the New York media devoured for five years like a hungry shark. And there's no denying the talent, which produced at least a share of four American League home run titles, six 100-RBI seasons, 12 All-Star Game appearances and a 1973 MVP award—a campaign in which he led Oakland to its second straight championship with a .293 average, 32 home runs and 117 RBIs.

Game 6 of the 1977 World Series was typical Jackson, who had endured a season of feuding with Yankees manager Billy Martin and several teammates, especially catcher Thurman Munson. Jackson, who already had hit two Series homers, dramatically powered three more—on consecutive pitches—in a Series-clinching victory over the Los Angeles Dodgers.

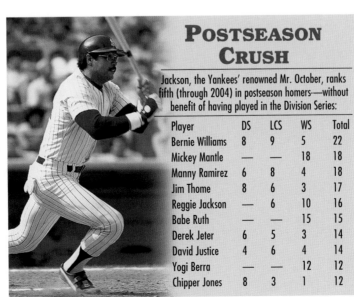

POSTSEASON CRUSH

Jackson, the Yankees' renowned Mr. October, ranks fifth (through 2004) in postseason homers—without benefit of having played in the Division Series:

Player	DS	LCS	WS	Total
Bernie Williams	8	9	5	22
Mickey Mantle	—	—	18	18
Manny Ramirez	6	8	4	18
Jim Thome	8	6	3	17
Reggie Jackson	—	6	10	16
Babe Ruth	—	—	15	15
Derek Jeter	6	5	3	14
David Justice	4	6	4	14
Yogi Berra	—	—	12	12
Chipper Jones	8	3	1	12

ROY 49 CAMPANELLA

C *1948-1957: DODGERS*

On one hand, the boyish enthusiasm that gushed from catcher Roy Campanella embodied the exciting, crazy Dodgers of the 1950s, Brooklyn's Boys of Summer. On the other hand, the same Campanella became the tragic symbol for a city's divorce from the team it had loved unconditionally for more than half a century. For 10 glorious seasons, Campy ruled the baseball world from his crouch

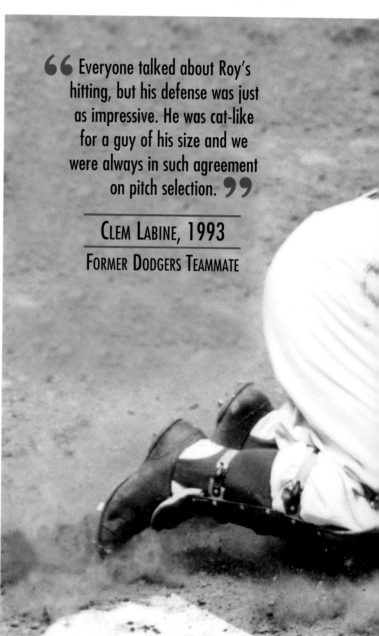

behind home plate. Then he spent the rest of his life in a wheelchair, the result of a crippling 1958 automobile accident.

The Campanella story is one of indomitable spirit. Following in the trail-blazing footsteps of Dodgers teammate Jackie Robinson, Campanella, who had started his professional career as a Negro League catcher at age 15, reported for major league duty in 1948 and quickly won over baseball-crazy Brooklyn fans. The combination of Campy's thick-necked, roly-poly build (5-foot-8, 200 pounds) and happy-go-lucky outlook was too much to resist.

So was the hustle, agility and cannon arm he displayed while challenging New York Yankees contemporary Yogi Berra for status as baseball's best catcher. Campanella was an adept handler of pitchers, agile and durable, a rock who could steady a sometimes erratic staff. And his quick, compact righthanded swing consistently muscled errant pitches into the left field stands at Ebbets Field.

How good was Campy? Three times in a five-year period he walked away with National League MVP awards, one following an incredible .312, 41-homer, 142-RBI 1953 campaign. His

Dodgers claimed five pennants and brought Brooklyn its first World Series crown; he played in seven All-Star Games.

Campanella, whose easygoing personality was a perfect fit for a difficult racial period, suffered a broken neck and paralysis in a January 1958 car accident—the

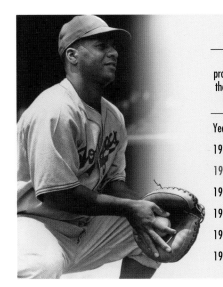

POWER PLUS

Campanella's 1953 MVP season was one of the most productive ever posted by a catcher. The following list shows the best home run totals through the 2005 season by players who worked at least 130 games behind the plate:

Year	Player/Team	HR	RBI
1970	Johnny Bench, Reds	45	148
1953	Roy Campanella, Dodgers	41	142
1996	Todd Hundley, Mets	41	112
1972	Johnny Bench, Reds	40	125
1997	Mike Piazza, Dodgers	40	124
1999	Mike Piazza, Dodgers	40	124

offseason before the Dodgers jilted Brooklyn fans with their cross-country move to Los Angeles. The wheelchair-confined Campy was elected to the Hall of Fame in 1969 and remained one of baseball's most gracious ambassadors until his death in 1993.

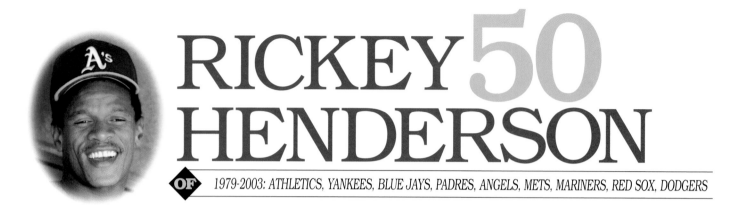

RICKEY 50
HENDERSON

H e was a merciless operative in cleats, bent on the destruction of every pitcher he met. It was nothing personal. Rickey Henderson just had a powerful obsession to get on base and score runs. When he achieved the first goal, the second usually followed, leaving a long trail of frazzled opponents in his speedy wake.

Henderson was the prototypical instigator, a talented leadoff man who changed the course of many games over his 25 major league seasons. He hit from an exaggerated righthanded crouch, daring pitchers to penetrate his Eddie Gaedel-like strike zone with a hittable pitch. If they didn't, he was perfectly happy with a walk that allowed him to exhibit his skills as the best basestealer in history. If they did, he was capable of launching the pitch 420 feet the other way. Among Henderson's 297 career home runs were 81—a big-league record—leading off the game.

The bottom line is that Henderson's career on-base percentage of .401 helped generate 1,406 stolen bases, a prodigious record fueled by the incredible 130 he swiped in 1982 and two other 100-steal seasons. The fleet left fielder led the American League in stolen bases 12 times, runs scored five times and walks on four occasions as the catalyst for nine teams— including four stints with Oakland and a 4½-year run with the New York Yankees. He also won a Gold Glove and provided the spark for three World Series teams, including winners in Oakland and Toronto.

STEALING THE SHOW

Henderson displayed his stolen base dominance by leading his league in that category a record 12 times. Here are players who have won or shared the most titles in several key offensive and pitching categories:

Category	Player
Average	Ty Cobb (12)
Runs	Babe Ruth (8)
Hits	Ty Cobb (8)
Home Runs	Babe Ruth (12)
RBIs	Babe Ruth (6)
Steals	Rickey Henderson (12)
Win Percentage	Lefty Grove (5)
ERA	Lefty Grove (9)
Strikeouts	Walter Johnson (12)

Henderson's offensive versatility did come with some baggage, however. The 10-time All-Star and 1990 A.L. MVP (for Oakland) played with a strutting arrogance that sometimes angered fans, opponents and even teammates. And he sometimes had to be prodded into giving his best effort or relinquishing his spot on the disabled list. But there was nothing unappealing about career numbers that include 3,055 hits, an all-time record of 2,295 runs scored, 2,190 walks (second in the record book) and a .279 career average through his final big-league season in 2003.

" He's the best leadoff hitter of all time, no question. There has never been a leadoff hitter who matched his combination of on-base percentage, basestealing ability and power. "

TONY KUBEK

LONGTIME PLAYER AND BROADCASTER
THE SPORTING NEWS, 1986

BIRTHPLACES

Alabama (5):
2. Willie Mays (Westfield)
5. Hank Aaron (Mobile)
21. Satchel Paige (Mobile)
55. Willie McCovey (Mobile)
89. Ozzie Smith (Mobile)

Arkansas (3):
58. Lou Brock (El Dorado)
82. Brooks Robinson (Little Rock)
88. Dizzy Dean (Lucas)

California (12):
6. Barry Bonds (Riverside)
9. Ted Williams (San Diego)
12. Joe DiMaggio (Martinez)
34. Tom Seaver (Fresno)
53. Harry Heilmann (San Francisco)
57. Tony Gwynn (Los Angeles)
60. Randy Johnson (Walnut Creek)
75. Lefty Gomez (Rodeo)
80. Eddie Murray (Los Angeles)
84. Mark McGwire (Pomona)
86. Duke Snider (Los Angeles)
99. Dennis Eckersley (Oakland)

Florida (1):
32. Steve Carlton (Miami)

Georgia (4):
3. Ty Cobb (Narrows)
20. Josh Gibson (Buena Vista)
44. Jackie Robinson (Cairo)
59. Bill Terry (Atlanta)

Idaho (1):
71. Harmon Killebrew (Payette)

Illinois (2):
50. Rickey Henderson (Chicago)
76. Robin Roberts (Springfield)

Indiana (2):
68. Oscar Charleston (Indianapolis)
92. Chuck Klein (Indianapolis)

Iowa (1):
37. Bob Feller (Van Meter)

Kansas (1):
4. Walter Johnson (Humboldt)

Louisiana (2):
42. Mel Ott (Gretna)
56. Bill Dickey (Bastrop)

Maryland (5):
1. Babe Ruth (Baltimore)
17. Jimmie Foxx (Sudlersville)
25. Lefty Grove (Lonaconing)
78. Al Kaline (Baltimore)
79. Cal Ripken (Havre de Grace)

Massachusetts (2):
66. Mickey Cochrane (Bridgewater)
72. Pie Traynor (Framingham)

Michigan (1):
46. Charley Gehringer (Fowlerville)

Minnesota (2):
96. Dave Winfield (St. Paul)
100. Paul Molitor (St. Paul)

Mississippi (1):
67. Cool Papa Bell (Starkville)

Payette (71)

Harmon Killebrew

Elba (13)   Omaha (33,
Wahoo (87)

Rodeo (75)   Martinez (12)
Walnut Creek (60)
San Francisco (53)   Oakland (99)

Fresno (34)

Mark McGwire

Oklahoma City (18)

Los Angeles(57, 80, 86)   Pomona (84)
Riverside (6)
San Diego (9)

Santa Rita (91)   Dallas (39)

Winters (10)
San Angelo (51)

Puerto Rico

Carolina (22)

Roberto Clemente

Gatún (62)

Panama

St. Paul (96, 100)

Buffalo (23)

Mickey Cochrane

Framingham (72) Bridgewater (66)

Woonsocket (31)

New York
(7, 28, 38, 52,
65, 70, 77, 90)

Millerton (26)

Southampton (74)

Milwaukee (43)

Fowlerville (46)

Factoryville (8)

Pequannock (97)

Plains (85)

Carteret (81)

Chicago (50)

Manchester (35)

Chartiers (14)

Philadelphia (49)

an Meter (37)

Donora (11, 93)

Gettysburg (69)

Wyncote (48)

Gilmore (16)

Dayton (15, 30)

Baltimore (1, 78)

Havre de Grace (79)

Lonaconing (25)

Sudlersville (17)

Springfield (76)

Indianapolis
(68, 92)

Cincinnati (27)

Glendale (54)

St. Louis (40)

Yogi Berra

oldt (4)

Carthage (45)

Rocky Mount (47)

Williamston (98)

Spavinaw (19)

(63)

Lucas (88)

Pickens County (36)

pro (83)

Little Rock (82)

Westfield (2)

Narrows (3)

Atlanta (59)

Josh Gibson

um (61)

Starkville (67)

Buena Vista (20)

El Dorado (58)

exarkana (64)

rd (29)

Bastrop (56)

Cairo (44)

Mobile (5, 21, 55, 89)

Gretna (42)

Beaumont (24)

o (41)

Miami (32)

United States

Laguna Verde (73)

Sammy Sosa

San Pedro de Macorís (95)

Dominican Republic

Missouri (2):
40. Yogi Berra (St. Louis)
45. Carl Hubbell (Carthage)

Nebraska (4):
13. Grover Alexander (Elba)
33. Bob Gibson (Omaha)
87. Sam Crawford (Wahoo)
94. Wade Boggs (Omaha)

New Jersey (2):
81. Joe Medwick (Carteret)
97. Derek Jeter (Pequannock)

New Mexico (1):
91. Ralph Kiner (Santa Rita)

New York (11):
7. Lou Gehrig (New York City)
23. Warren Spahn (Buffalo)
26. Eddie Collins (Millerton)
28. Sandy Koufax (Brooklyn)
38. Hank Greenberg (New York City)
52. Whitey Ford (New York City)
65. Jim Palmer (New York City)
70. Alex Rodriguez (New York City)
74. Carl Yastrzemski (Southampton)
77. Willie Keeler (Brooklyn)
90. Frank Frisch (Bronx)

North Carolina (2):
47. Buck Leonard (Rocky Mount)
98. Gaylord Perry (Williamston)

Ohio (5):
15. Roger Clemens (Dayton)
16. Cy Young (Gilmore)
27. Pete Rose (Cincinnati)
30. Mike Schmidt (Dayton)
35. George Sisler (Manchester)

Oklahoma (4):
18. Johnny Bench (Oklahoma City)
19. Mickey Mantle (Spavinaw)
63. Paul Waner (Harrah)
83. Willie Stargell (Earlsboro)

Pennsylvania (8):
8. Christy Mathewson (Factoryville)
11. Stan Musial (Donora)
14. Honus Wagner (Chartiers)
48. Reggie Jackson (Wyncote)
49. Roy Campanella (Philadelphia)
69. Eddie Plank (Gettysburg)
85. Ed Walsh (Plains)
93. Ken Griffey Jr. (Donora)

Rhode Island (1):
31. Napoleon Lajoie (Woonsocket)

South Carolina (1):
36. Joe Jackson (Pickens County)

Texas (8):
10. Rogers Hornsby (Winters)
24. Frank Robinson (Beaumont)
29. Tris Speaker (Hubbard)
39. Ernie Banks (Dallas)
41. Nolan Ryan (Refugio)
51. Greg Maddux (San Angelo)
61. Joe Morgan (Bonham)
64. Eddie Mathews (Texarkana)

West Virginia (1):
54. George Brett (Glendale)

Wisconsin (1):
43. Al Simmons (Milwaukee)

Other (4):
22. Roberto Clemente (Carolina, Puerto Rico)
62. Rod Carew (Gatun, Canal Zone, Panama)
73. Juan Marichal (Laguna Verde, Dominican Republic)
95. Sammy Sosa (San Pedro De Macoris, Dom. Rep.)

> " Greg Maddux is truly an artist.
> When I watch Greg Maddux, he is
> all I wish I could have been. "
>
> DON SUTTON, 1996

GREG 51 MADDUX

P *1986-PRESENT: CUBS, BRAVES*

He's equal parts scientist, artist and magician, a professorial-looking righthander with the ability to dissect a lineup, paint a corner or make a good hitter disappear. Greg Maddux is a throwback. He's an efficiency expert, an old-style craftsman who kills opponents softly with his masterful control, deceptive cunning and rally-stopping defense.

For two decades, every Maddux performance has been a clinic. Cut fastball outside corner. Slider inside. Curveball, cut fastball, changeup—everything in its place, hitters always off-balance. Maddux has the uncanny ability to throw any pitch anywhere he wants on any count. Hitters, seldom in sync with the pitch, usually reach or get handcuffed, resulting in a harmless grounder or fly ball. Location and pitch movement—those are the magic words that give him status among the most successful pitchers of his era.

During his prime—seven career-opening seasons with the Chicago Cubs and 11 more as ace of the Atlanta Braves—a typical Maddux outing often ended in about two hours with him throwing fewer than 100 pitches. He seldom walked a hitter and sometimes played with him—like a cat with a mouse. When in trouble, he helped himself with a defensive genius that earned him 13 con-secutive Gold Gloves, 14 overall. During his years in Atlanta, the Braves never failed to win a division title and appeared in three World Series, winning one.

Maddux's all-around consistency is amazing. In 2004, making a triumphant return to the Cubs, he became the 22nd pitcher in baseball's elite 300-win club, and his 16 victories stretched his unprecedented streak of 15-win seasons to 17. Twice he has won 20 games; five times he has recorded 19 wins in a season. From 1992—his last year in his first tour with the Cubs—through 1995, Maddux forged records of 20-11 (2.18 ERA), 20-10 (2.36), 16-6 (1.56) and 19-2 (1.63) and won the N.L. Cy Young Award each season. The durable righthander, who never has missed time with an arm ailment, has made 33 or more starts in every non-strike season beginning in 1988.

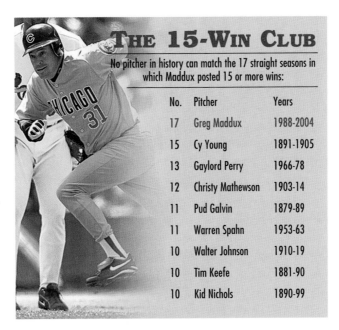

THE 15-WIN CLUB

No pitcher in history can match the 17 straight seasons in which Maddux posted 15 or more wins:

No.	Pitcher	Years
17	Greg Maddux	1988-2004
15	Cy Young	1891-1905
13	Gaylord Perry	1966-78
12	Christy Mathewson	1903-14
11	Pud Galvin	1879-89
11	Warren Spahn	1953-63
10	Walter Johnson	1910-19
10	Tim Keefe	1881-90
10	Kid Nichols	1890-99

WHITEY FORD 52

He may not have been baseball's original "crafty little lefthander," but Whitey Ford sure fit the description as well as anybody who pitched before or after him. The blond-headed, 5-foot-10, 180-pound New Yorker also was the ace for a New York Yankees juggernaut that captured 11 American League pennants and six World Series titles with him at the pitching controls between 1950 and 1964.

What Ford's left arm lacked in power his head made up for with guile, determination and instinct. He delivered his fastball, curve, sinker and slider with overhand, three-quarters and sidearm motions, rarely giving the hitter the same look on consecutive pitches. His control was outstanding; his confident demeanor never wavered; his pickoff move froze embarrassed baserunners, and his bulldog determination seemed to toughen as the situation warranted.

Supported by a series of powerful Yankees lineups, Ford parlayed his pitching prowess into an incredible .690 career winning percentage, the best in major league history for a 200-game winner. His 25-4 record earned him a 1961 Cy Young Award and he posted ERA titles in 1956 and 1958. His 236-106 career mark could have been even better if not for the two peak seasons (1951 and '52) he lost to military service during the Korean War.

Ford, praised by longtime manager Casey Stengel as the best money pitcher in baseball, was at his best in postseason play. He still holds World Series records for wins (10), strikeouts (94), games (22) and innings pitched (146) and he once worked a fall classic-record 33 straight scoreless innings. His two shutouts in a 1961 five-game win over Cincinnati earned him MVP honors.

Ford, a six-time All-Star Game performer who threw 45 career shutouts, was known for his sense of humor and the clever one-line quips that brought back memories of Hall of Famer Lefty Gomez among longtime Yankee fans. He also was known for the nightlife he enjoyed to extremes with longtime friends and teammates Mickey Mantle and Billy Martin.

WINNING FORMULA

Ford was a key figure for 11 pennant winners and six World Series champions in the 1950s and '60s. His regular-season records and winning percentage convey his importance to the title teams:

Yr.	Record	Pct.
1950	9-1	.900
1953	18-6	.750
1956	19-6	.760
1958	14-7	.667
1961	25-4	.862
1962	17-8	.680
Total	102-32	.761

"You go up to the plate thinking confidently that this is the time I'm going to do well against (Ford). Trouble is, you never seem to do it. "

BROOKS ROBINSON

THE SPORTING NEWS, 1964

> 66 People nowadays just don't realize how great a
> hitter Harry was. Next to Rogers Hornsby, he
> was the best righthanded hitter of them all. 99

TY COBB

THE SPORTING NEWS, 1951

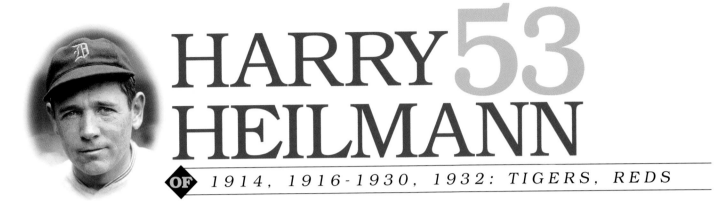

HARRY 53
HEILMANN

OF *1914, 1916-1930, 1932: TIGERS, REDS*

He was slow afoot, his defense was sometimes suspect and his personality was overshadowed by Detroit outfield partner Ty Cobb. But, oh, could Harry Heilmann hit! He proved that over 17 major league seasons, competing with the likes of Cobb, Rogers Hornsby, George Sisler, Babe Ruth, Tris Speaker and Lou Gehrig for batting superiority in the 1920s.

"Old Slug," a nickname bestowed by Heilmann's Detroit teammates because of his lack of speed, was a 6-foot-1 righthanded hitter who slashed line drives around American League ballparks with alarming frequency from 1914-32. He attacked the pitch from a slight crouch and moved his hands up and down the bat, one of many hitting tricks he learned from Cobb in his formative years. Heilmann never ranked high on the home run charts (his best season was 21), but he consistently showed up among leaders in doubles and triples and he topped the 100-RBI plateau eight times in a productive nine-season span.

Heilmann's legacy will always be his bat and nothing personifies hitting excellence more than the four A.L. batting titles he captured in the decade of the hitter—with lofty averages of .394 (1921), .403 (1923), .393 (1925) and .398 (1927). He was only nine well-placed hits away from being a four-time .400 hitter and his career .342 average ranks among the top 10 all-time. Heilmann cranked out 2,660 hits, the final 161 of which came with the Cincinnati Reds over his last two seasons.

The personable, outgoing Heilmann was a longtime favorite of Detroit fans, who needed him as a buffer for their long-standing love/hate relationship with the controversial Cobb. Long after retirement in 1932, Heilmann remained a close personal friend of both Cobb and Ruth, two of the game's most colorful and divergent personalities.

Heilmann, who never played for a Detroit pennant-winner, was no longer around to savor the moment when his Hall of Fame election was announced in 1952. He had died seven months earlier of lung cancer.

THE SEARCH FOR .400

Heilmann won four every-other-year batting titles in the 1920s. The following chart shows how nine more well-placed hits would have given him additional distinction as the only player to top the magic .400 mark four times:

Year	AB	Hits	Avg.	Needed for .400
1921	602	237	.394	4
1923	524	211	.403	0
1925	573	225	.393	4
1927	505	201	.398	1

GEORGE BRETT 54

The first thing pitchers noticed about George Brett was the concentration, the intense eye contact that suggested he was up for any challenge. The second was one of his line drives plugging the gap or nestling into either corner, a likely occurrence with a game on the line. Brett was known for many magical moments during his 21-season run with the Kansas City Royals, but his

reputation as one of the most feared clutch hitters in history is his baseball legacy.

He broke into the major leagues in 1973 as a sure-handed but scatter-armed third baseman and finished his career 3,154 hits later as a first baseman. The sandy-haired, free-spirited Californian credited his offensive prowess, which produced 1,119 extra-base hits and American League batting titles in three different decades, to hitting guru Charley Lau, who changed him from a Carl Yastrzemski-type free swinger into a controlled, weight-shifting machine.

The sight of the lefthanded-hitting Brett crouching, weight shifted to the back leg and bat resting comfortably on his shoulder, suggested confidence and relaxed control. His focus was unbreakable, his swing was picture-perfect and he always was a step ahead of the pitcher. He could drive the ball with power to any section of the park and his flair for dramatics was uncanny.

Numerous big-game home runs and his post-season passion attest to that. So does an MVP-winning 1980 season in which Brett batted .390 and drove in 118 runs in 117 games. He also is

> 66 George is the best player in the American League. He's hard-nosed, he's aggressive and he's instinctive. He has the best physical and mental makeup of any player in the game. 99

JIM FREY, 1980
FORMER ROYALS MANAGER

FACE OF A FRANCHISE

No player dominates a franchise's record book more than Brett, who is the Royals' career leader in every meaningful offensive category except stolen bases. And he ranks fourth in steals:

Games	2,707
At-Bats	10,349
Runs	1,583
Hits	3,154
Doubles	665
Triples	137
Home runs	317
Total bases	5,044
RBIs	1,595
Extra-base hits	1,119
Batting average	.305
Stolen bases	201 (4th)

remembered for his A.L. Championship Series heroics against the New York Yankees—a dramatic Game 5 home run in 1976, a three-homer game in 1978, a pennant-securing homer in 1980—as well as the infamous 1983 "Pine Tar" homer he belted at Yankee Stadium.

Brett, a .373 hitter in two World Series and a 10-time All-Star Game participant, could have posted even better numbers if not for a series of nagging injuries, the product of the aggressive, hustling intensity he always brought to the field.

"You've got to fear McCovey more than you do a .340 or .350 hitter when he's in position to bat in the winning or tying run. I think you could hurt the Giants if you walked McCovey every time he came up."

SPARKY ANDERSON

THE SPORTING NEWS, 1973

WILLIE 55 McCOVEY

1B *1959-1980: GIANTS, PADRES, ATHLETICS*

Cincinnati manager Sparky Anderson called him "the most awesome man I've ever seen." Pitchers shuddered and an expectant hush enveloped the ballpark every time he stepped into the batter's box. Intimidation really wasn't Willie McCovey's style, but you couldn't convince fans or opponents who watched him stage consistently spectacular power displays over a 22-year major league career that started in 1959 and touched four decades.

In reality, the 6-foot-4, 220-pound San Francisco first baseman was a gentle Giant, amiable, soft-spoken and always respectful. But at the plate, the towering lefthanded hitter was the epitome of intimidation—massive arms sweeping a toothpick-like bat back and forth, dipping it menacingly low, as the pitcher released the ball. He didn't just hit home runs; he launched them high and far with a whiplash swing that produced 521, as well as three National League homer crowns.

McCovey is best remembered as the enforcer who protected Willie Mays for 13-plus seasons in the Giants' lineup (they combined for 814 home runs) and the man who hit the blistering line drive that New York Yankees second baseman Bobby Richardson snared for the heart-breaking final

out in Game 7 of the 1962 World Series. But the man teammates called "Stretch" also was a solid first baseman, a three-time slugging percentage leader and a .270 career hitter who earned an MVP award in 1969—a season in which he batted .320 with 45 homers and 126 RBIs while drawing a record 45 intentional walks.

McCovey, a six-time All-Star Game performer who hit two home runs in the 1969 midsummer classic, might have posted even bigger career numbers if not for some physical problems nobody could see. He played his entire career without complaint on arthritic, surgically repaired knees that hindered his running and quick movement and he later battled other injuries and intense back problems. McCovey retired in 1980 with 18 career grand slams, second at the time only to Lou Gehrig's still-standing record of 23.

LIFE IS GRAND

McCovey is tied for fourth on the all-time grand-slam list:

Player	Slams
Lou Gehrig	23
Manny Ramirez	20
Eddie Murray	19
Willie McCovey	18
Robin Ventura	18
Jimmie Foxx	17
Ted Williams	17
Hank Aaron	16
Dave Kingman	16
Babe Ruth	16

There is only one Bill Dickey. Bill isn't fast. But he is the best handler of pitchers I ever saw. Beyond which, he is the greatest clutch hitter I ever saw, not only for a catcher but for anyone else in baseball. "

ROGER BRESNAHAN
HALL OF FAME CATCHER

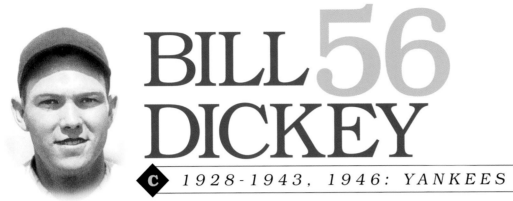

BILL 56 DICKEY

C   1928-1943, 1946: YANKEES

He fit into his catching gear as naturally as a turtle into its shell. When Bill Dickey crouched behind the plate, all was right in Yankeeland and pennant-crazy New York fans could thank the baseball gods that their pitching staff was in good hands. Dickey lived up to his part of that bond for 17 major league seasons as a link between the Ruth/Gehrig/Lazzeri champions of the late 1920s and the DiMaggio/Keller/Gordon winning machines of the late 1930s and early '40s.

Before heading off to war in 1944, Dickey backstopped eight New York pennant winners and seven World Series champs, a legacy he passed on in 1946 to rookie Yogi Berra, who would catch 14 pennant-winners and 10 champions of his own. The stately Dickey provided an interesting contrast as tutor to the roly-poly Berra, but both men moved around behind the plate with similar cat-like quickness, authority and agility. No one, however, could match Dickey's tactical genius and ability to keep pitchers on an even keel.

Few catchers, before or since, have been able to match Dickey's dangerous bat, either. A 10-time .300 hitter who sprayed hits all over the park from his upright lefthanded stance, he was especially dangerous in the clutch. Not surprisingly, the four consecutive 100-RBI seasons he strung together from 1936-39 coincided with four straight Yankees World Series wins, a then-unprecedented achievement. Dickey's signature fall classic moment came in 1943, when he decided the Game 5 finale against St. Louis with a two-run homer.

But Dickey, who played in eight All-Star Games, is best remembered for a rugged durability that allowed him to catch 100-plus games in 13 straight seasons and a surprising 1932 incident in which the quiet, mild-mannered catcher delivered a one-punch knockout to Washington's Carl Reynolds after a home-plate collision, breaking his jaw and drawing a 30-day suspension. More significant was his introduction of a smaller, lightweight catcher's mitt that helped revolutionize the position.

HIGH SOCIETY

Dickey still ranked among the top 10 all-time Yankees in numerous offensive categories through 2005:

Category	Rank	Total
Games	7th	1,789
At-Bats	10th	6,300
Hits	8th	1,969
Doubles	7th	343
Triples	T9th	72
Home Runs	11th	202
Total Bases	8th	3,062
RBIs	6th	1,209
Extra-base Hits	8th	617
Batting Average	7th	.313

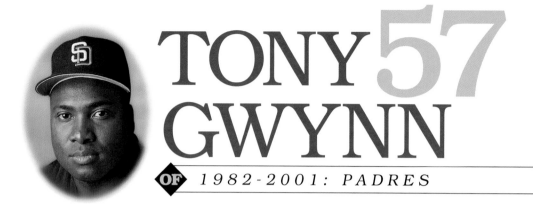

TONY 57 GWYNN

He has been called the best pure hitter since Ted Williams. And his eight National League batting championships put him in the exclusive company of Ty Cobb (the only major leaguer to win more titles) and Honus Wagner (whose N.L. record he tied). The national attention that could have eluded Tony Gwynn—he was the 20-year centerpiece for the small-market San Diego Padres—was earned the hard way, with hundreds of average-inflating line drives into the gap.

Gwynn was baseball's consummate batsman of the 1990s, a Williams/Cobb-like connoisseur who carefully molded his crouching, left-handed swing and studied his craft with a scientific fervor. Not only was Gwynn a master at using the entire field, he was a superb two-strike hitter, a durable model of consistency and a feared clutch hitter who posted 3,141 hits and a career .338 average. The portly right fielder topped the .300 mark in each of the 19 seasons he played after his 1982 debut, and he posted five straight .350-plus seasons from 1993-97. Gwynn was one of the first players to hone his swing with extensive use of video tapes.

Gwynn, who never went more than 19 at-bats without a hit, was a pitcher's worst enemy, even as his 5-11 frame ballooned to 225 pounds and knee problems reduced the steal threat he once posed on the bases. And he never lost the infectious enthusiasm he brought to the locker room or the attention to detail he brought to the field. Gwynn attacked

> 66 Gwynn is the Picasso of modern-day hitters. Nobody studies the game harder, pays more attention to detail and goes to the plate with a better idea of what he wants to do. 99
>
> TED WILLIAMS

his job with passion, whether playing solid defense that earned him five Gold Gloves, moving runners with a grounder to the right side or delivering hits with assembly-line consistency.

Gwynn's hitting prowess was only part of the legacy he left Padres fans when he retired in 2001. The former San Diego State basketball and baseball star was a big part of the team's only two National League pennants (1984 and 1998) and, easily, the most beloved player in franchise history. He also was a 13-time All-Star Game participant who ranks among the most enthusiastic, accessible and popular players of his era.

STREAKING

When Gwynn completed the 1997 campaign with a .372 average, he became only the fourth player in history to record five consecutive .350-plus seasons:

Player/Team	.350 Streak	Yrs.
Ty Cobb, Tigers	11	1909-19
Rogers Hornsby, Cards	6	1920-25
Tony Gwynn, Padres	5	1993-97
Al Simmons, Athletics	5	1927-31
George Sisler, Browns	4	1919-22
Tris Speaker, Indians	4	1920-23
Wade Boggs, Red Sox	4	1985-88

"You look at Lou's career and you envy it. I do. I think most players do."

TED SIMMONS

BROCK'S LONGTIME TEAMMATE
THE SPORTING NEWS, 1979

LOU 58 BROCK

His big smile, soft voice and slow, graceful movements belied the thievery in Lou Brock's heart. His thoughtful, analytical mind meticulously planned the controlled mayhem he would perpetrate on helpless pitchers and defenders. The stolen base was Brock's weapon and he dominated games throughout the 1960s and '70s without even touching a bat, ball or glove.

Brock, a reliable left fielder with good range, was the ultimate leadoff man and driving force for the St. Louis Cardinals in an era that featured long-ball hitters, one-base-at-a-time strategy and dominant pitchers. He was a dangerous lefthanded batter who slashed out 3,023 hits, but the real damage Brock inflicted came after he had reached base. Using his outstanding speed like a club, he pounded away at distracted pitchers while setting a new course for baseball strategy.

If the stolen base was Brock's artform, then the 1974 season was his masterpiece. His .306 average and 194 hits set the tone for a startling 118-stolen base performance—14 steals better than the record-setting Maury Wills total of 1962. Brock taking a short lead, sprinting for second and arriving safely with a quick pop-up slide was a familiar sight throughout National League cities.

It wasn't as easy as it looked. Brock spent hours studying pitchers, timing their deliveries and moves to first base. He approached hitting in the same meticulous manner and his work ethic paid dividends. Eight times he batted .300 and four times he reached the 200-hit plateau. Brock, a trade acquisition from the Chicago Cubs in 1964, scored 90 or more runs 10 times—in close correlation to his eight stolen base titles.

A five-time All-Star Game performer who sparked the Cardinals to three pennants and two World Series titles in the 1960s, Brock batted .391 with 34 hits and 13 RBIs in fall classic play. His final signature on a Hall of Fame career came in 1979 when he became baseball's all-time leading basestealer—a plateau he reached with then record-setting steal No. 938.

STOLEN MEMORIES

When Brock stole his record-setting 118 bases in 1974, Davey Lopes, his nearest major league competitor, checked in with half that total. That's the second-biggest first/second differential in baseball's eight 100-steal seasons:

Year	Leader/Total	2nd/Total
1962	Maury Wills, 104	Willie Davis, 32
1974	Lou Brock, 118	Davey Lopes, 59
1982	Rickey Henderson, 130	Tim Raines, 78
1987	Vince Coleman, 109	Harold Reynolds, 60
1985	Vince Coleman, 110	Rickey Henderson, 80
1986	Vince Coleman, 107	Rickey Henderson, 87
1983	Rickey Henderson, 108	Tim Raines, 90
1980	Rickey Henderson, 100	Ron LeFlore, 97

“Bill managed like he played. It was business to him, not fun, and he was successful.”

CARL HUBBELL, 1948

BILL 59 TERRY

The first thing you noticed about Bill Terry was the hard-edged bluntness, a glassy-eyed, no-nonsense attitude that made it perfectly clear he was about business, not pleasure. Baseball was a means to Terry's end and he pulled no punches in his legendary duels with strong-willed New York Giants manager John McGraw, his frank dealings with members of the press and his no-mercy plundering of National League pitchers.

Terry grew up in poverty, the victim of a broken home in Jacksonville, Fla., and his silent rage and obsession to succeed were magnified with every line drive he slashed into the spacious left and right-center field gaps at New York's Polo Grounds. His aloofness in the locker room transformed into competitive passion when he took the field and that passion was documented by the .341 average the graceful 6-foot-2, 200-pound first baseman carved out over a 14-year major league career.

Terry's icy glare and savage line drives through the box unnerved many pitchers, who feared the straightaway hitting style of the powerfully built, shoulder-hunching left-hander. His third New York season in 1925 produced a .319 average and he failed to top the .300 plateau only once

over the next 11 years. He was a machine-like batsman who piled up six 200-hit seasons and topped 100 RBIs seven times. Terry's signature performance came in 1930 when he amassed 254 hits and posted an eye-catching .401 average that still stands as the last .400 season in N.L. history.

The Terry-McGraw personality clashes were legendary—they once went a year and a half without speaking to each other. But when McGraw suddenly ended his brilliant 33-year managerial run in 1932, he handpicked Terry as his successor. It was a prudent choice.

As player-manager, Terry guided the Giants to two pennants and a 1933 World Series victory over the Washington Senators. He retired from active duty after the 1936 season, but continued in his managerial capacity until 1941, leading the Giants to one more pennant in 1937.

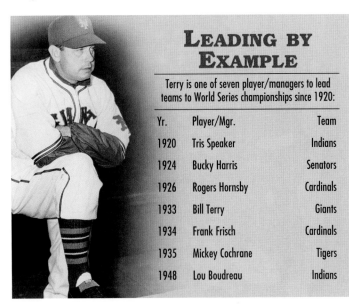

LEADING BY EXAMPLE

Terry is one of seven player/managers to lead teams to World Series championships since 1920:

Yr.	Player/Mgr.	Team
1920	Tris Speaker	Indians
1924	Bucky Harris	Senators
1926	Rogers Hornsby	Cardinals
1933	Bill Terry	Giants
1934	Frank Frisch	Cardinals
1935	Mickey Cochrane	Tigers
1948	Lou Boudreau	Indians

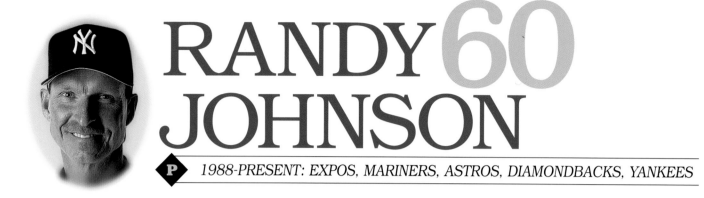

RANDY 60
JOHNSON

P *1988-PRESENT: EXPOS, MARINERS, ASTROS, DIAMONDBACKS, YANKEES*

The menacing scowl and "make my day" glare test the willpower of accomplished major league hitters, even before Randy Johnson slings all 6 feet, 10 inches of his 231-pound body homeward, along with a 99-mph fastball. Eyes widen, knees buckle and intestinal fortitude suffers with each of the 100-plus deliveries the Big Unit makes in a typical start. And, not surprisingly, fear often strikes out against one of the most intimidating left-handers in baseball history.

The "intimidation factor" has only grown over Johnson's 18-year major league career, which started inauspiciously in 1988 at Montreal when the awkward 25-year-old struggled to get his pitches over the plate. In succeeding stops at Seattle, Houston, Arizona and with the New York Yankees, he blossomed into baseball's Big Unit, the most overpowering lefty strikeout artist and intimidator since Dodgers great Sandy Koufax in the 1960s.

Few pitchers have made such a lasting impression on managers, who invariably "rest" their top lefthanded hitters against Johnson. If not, he can embarrass them with a flailing delivery and a steady diet of exploding fast-balls, two-seamers and sweeping sliders. Nine times he has led his league in strikeouts. Once he struck out a record-tying 20 batters in the first nine innings of an 11-inning game; twice he has fanned 19. His 10.95 strikeouts per nine innings is the best ratio of all-time.

Johnson's career winning percentage of .659 (through 2005) also ranks among the best all-time, and his 263 career win total is nearing elite territory. Season records of 18-2, 20-4, 21-6 and 24-5 attest to his dominance, as does his 3.11 career ERA and five Cy Young Awards. Only 2-7 in Division Series play through 2004, Johnson led Arizona's championship charge in 2001 with a 3-0 record and 1.04 ERA in a World Series win over the Yankees.

Like good wine, Johnson ages well. Working for the Diamondbacks at 40, he became the oldest pitcher to throw a perfect game (his second career no-hitter), and he turned 42 near the end of a 2005 campaign in which he went 17-8 as a first-year Yankee.

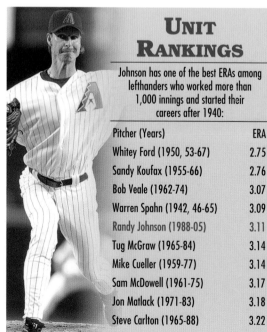

UNIT RANKINGS

Johnson has one of the best ERAs among lefthanders who worked more than 1,000 innings and started their careers after 1940:

Pitcher (Years)	ERA
Whitey Ford (1950, 53-67)	2.75
Sandy Koufax (1955-66)	2.76
Bob Veale (1962-74)	3.07
Warren Spahn (1942, 46-65)	3.09
Randy Johnson (1988-05)	3.11
Tug McGraw (1965-84)	3.14
Mike Cueller (1959-77)	3.14
Sam McDowell (1961-75)	3.17
Jon Matlack (1971-83)	3.18
Steve Carlton (1965-88)	3.22

◆ SPORTING NEWS SELECTS BASEBALL'S 100 GREATEST PLAYERS ◆

"I can't compare him to my era. But I know he'd be good in any era. He's head and shoulders above everyone else."

WARREN SPAHN
THE SPORTING NEWS, 2002

> **" When he's healthy, he's the finest ballplayer I ever played with. He could win more ballgames in more ways than anybody. "**
>
> JOHNNY BENCH, 1980

JOE 61 MORGAN

2B *1963-1984: COLT .45s/ASTROS, REDS, GIANTS, PHILLIES, ATHLETICS*

He was an equal-opportunity assassin. Joe Morgan could kill you softly with his glove, speed and quick mind. Or he could kill you savagely with a vicious line drive into the gap or a heart-piercing home run. Either way, you always wound up dead and Morgan wound up another step closer to the Hall of Fame.

That lofty height must have seemed out of reach for the 5-foot-7, 155-pound second baseman when he made his major league debut with Houston in 1963. But Morgan used his quick hands, analytical approach and game-turning speed to wreak a special kind of havoc. By the time he was traded to Cincinnati in November 1971, he was a well-oiled generator for a Big Red Machine that was ready to run roughshod through the National League.

"Little Joe," who was called the "strongest little guy I've ever been around" by former manager Sparky Anderson, was at his best from 1972 through 1977 when he helped the Reds capture four division titles and consecutive World Series. He won five Gold Gloves and averaged .301 with 113 runs, 118 walks, 22 home runs, 84 RBIs and 60 stolen bases over that six-year stretch while earning back-to-back MVPs. The articulate, quick-to-laugh Morgan, who decided the '75 fall classic with a ninth-inning Game 7 single, simply did whatever it took to win, as illustrated by his 1976 MVP numbers—.320, 27 homers, 111 RBIs, 113 runs, 114 walks and 60 steals.

Morgan, a lefthanded hitter who distinctively flapped his left elbow before every pitch, showed a Ted Williams-like patience that allowed him to set an N.L. career record for walks (since broken by Barry Bonds) with 1,865. But he swung often enough to rap out 2,517 hits and 268 home runs while posting eight 100-run seasons and stealing 689 bases.

Morgan's bottom line, however, was winning. The nine-time All-Star Game performer played for seven division titlists, four pennant-winners and two Series champions. His last fall classic appearance came with Philadelphia in 1983—the second-to-last season in a 22-year career.

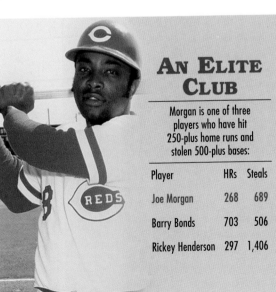

AN ELITE CLUB

Morgan is one of three players who have hit 250-plus home runs and stolen 500-plus bases:

Player	HRs	Steals
Joe Morgan	268	689
Barry Bonds	703	506
Rickey Henderson	297	1,406

" I've never seen anyone quite like this fellow. I saw Ted Williams do things with a baseball bat I'd never seen done before. I never thought I'd see better, but that was before I saw Carew. "

GENE MAUCH, 1977

ROD **62** CAREW

He handled the bat with the same efficiency Merlin coaxed from his wand. Rod Carew was a baseball magician with the power to make well-placed pitches disappear into every conceivable outfield gap. Carew was to the 1970s what Ty Cobb was to the 1910s and Rogers Hornsby to the 1920s—a bat-control artist, the keeper of batting titles and an annual threat to hit .400.

Carew performed his magic from an exaggerated crouch with a 32-ounce bat and a natural inside-out lefthanded swing that allowed him to stay back until the last possible second and spray line drives to all fields. He was selective and smart, an outstanding two-strike hitter with the speed to beat out infield hits and steal bases. Former manager Billy Martin marveled at Carew's bat-handling abilities ("he could bunt .330 if he tried") and instinctive baserunning after watching him swipe home seven times in an inspiring 1969 performance.

Such efficiency allowed him to win seven batting titles in 12 seasons with the Minnesota Twins—the first in his third big-league season (1969) and the other six in a seven-year period beginning in 1972. Carew, a career .328 hitter, never quite reached the .400

plateau that many predicted, but he did pull off a .388, 239-hit 1977 performance that earned him American League MVP honors. The slender Panamanian topped .300 15 times and .330 nine times while posting four 200-hit seasons.

Carew, young and unsure of his sudden celebrity, was a moody, sometimes-difficult locker room loner when he captured Rookie of the Year honors as an erratic Twins second baseman in 1967. But he was a well-respected veteran first baseman when he collected his 3,000th career hit in 1985, his seventh and final season with the California Angels. The only thing missing from Carew's Hall of Fame ledger was a World Series appearance, although he did play in four A.L. Championship Series—two each with the Twins and Angels—and 15 All-Star Games.

HIT MAN

The only thing that stood between Carew and a string of seven straight A.L. batting titles was George Brett in 1976. Ty Cobb is the only player to win more than six in a row:

Yr.	A.L. Leader
1972	Rod Carew, .318
1973	Rod Carew, .350
1974	Rod Carew, .364
1975	Rod Carew, .359
1976	George Brett, .333
	(Rod Carew, .331)
1977	Rod Carew, .388
1978	Rod Carew, .333

> " Paul was the greatest hitter I ever saw. They (Paul and Lloyd) were lefthanded hitters who hit to all fields, but everything Paul hit was a line drive. "

DICK BARTELL
FORMER PIRATES TEAMMATE

OF *1926-1945: PIRATES, DODGERS, BRAVES, YANKEES*

He was the marquee half of the most offensive brother act ever to take the baseball stage. Hits simply oozed out of Paul Waner's oversized bat, and all the leftovers he passed on to brother Lloyd. The sprightly Waner brothers, Paul in right and Lloyd in center, were like gnats buzzing the faces of National League pitchers for the 14 seasons (1927-40) they spent together as speedy flychasers in Pittsburgh's outfield.

The 5-foot-8½, 153-pound Paul (Big Poison) was a better hitter than his 5-8¼, 150-pound younger brother (Little Poison), but not by much. Lloyd, the Pirates' leadoff hitter, would slap a single and Paul would shoot a drive down the line or into a gap, scoring his brother or sending him to third. That combination carried the Pirates to the 1927 World Series, a classic they lost in four games to the powerful New York Yankees.

Paul was a lefthanded-swinging bat-control artist who stepped into the pitch from a close-footed stance, driving some balls to the opposite field, tomahawking others to right. He was fast enough to beat out infield rollers and quick enough to fend off the nastiest of pitches. Waner seldom struck out (34 times in his worst season) and managed eight 200-hit seasons, a figure topped only by Pete Rose and Ty Cobb. His three N.L. batting titles were the result of .380, .362 and .373 efforts.

Waner, who compiled 3,152 hits and a .333 average over 20 seasons, topped the .300 plateau in his first 12 years and earned the League MVP award in 1927 when he complemented his first batting title with a league-leading 18 triples and 131 RBIs. He also was an outstanding right fielder with speed, instincts and a strong, accurate arm.

Waner's only weakness was an affinity for the carousing nightlife that kept Yankees contemporary Babe Ruth in hot water. But it never seemed to affect Waner's performance or the scientific hitting approach he later passed on to Ted Williams and countless others who sought his batting counsel.

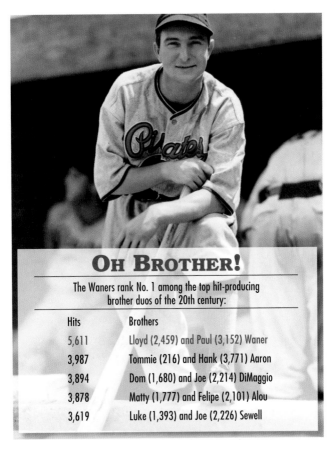

OH BROTHER!

The Waners rank No. 1 among the top hit-producing brother duos of the 20th century:

Hits	Brothers
5,611	Lloyd (2,459) and Paul (3,152) Waner
3,987	Tommie (216) and Hank (3,771) Aaron
3,894	Dom (1,680) and Joe (2,214) DiMaggio
3,878	Matty (1,777) and Felipe (2,101) Alou
3,619	Luke (1,393) and Joe (2,226) Sewell

EDDIE 64
MATHEWS

3B *1952-1968: BRAVES, ASTROS, TIGERS*

The apple cheeks, dark, handsome features and Texas country-boy shyness belied the quick temper and fiery intensity Eddie Mathews brought to a diamond. So did the boyish charm that captivated fans and the mesmerizing swing that tortured pitchers for 17 major league seasons. Eddie Mathews was a baseball enigma—a sleek, fast, hungry wildcat disguised as a mild-mannered, power-hitting third baseman for the Boston/Milwaukee/Atlanta Braves.

Mathews' 6-foot-1, 200-pound, rock-solid body was a near perfect blend of speed, quickness and power. The speed was documented in 1953, his second season, when he was timed from home to first in 3.5 seconds. The quickness was critical to Mathews' development as a solid third baseman and his near-perfect lefthanded swing, which launched 512 home runs.

Early observers saw a lot of Ted Williams in Mathews' batting style. He used a slightly open stance to attack pitches with a buggy-whip swing that shot line drives into distant stands. A dead-pull hitter who powered home runs in bunches, he formed a lethal 13-season combination in the Braves' lineup with Hank Aaron. Four times he powered 40-plus homers, 10 times he topped 30 while driving in 1,453 runs. The Aaron-Mathews tandem led Milwaukee to consecutive pennants and the city's only championship in 1957.

Mathews was an instant favorite of fans who watched him bat .302 with 47 homers and 135 RBIs in 1953—the Braves' first Milwaukee season. That was Mathews' way of signaling elite status among such contemporary sluggers as Aaron, Mickey Mantle, Willie Mays, Duke Snider and Ralph Kiner. In the eight-year stretch from 1953-60, he averaged 39 homers and 105 RBIs while consistently ranking among league leaders in walks and runs scored.

The sometimes-moody Mathews, who won two home run crowns and played in 10 All-Star Games, was feared beyond his hitting feats. His fiery temper was exhibited in several celebrated baseball fights—none of which he lost. But former teammates cited the never-say-die hustle, personal expectations and demands he made on others as the real bottom line.

POWER PACKS

Aaron and Mathews, who were teammates with the Milwaukee and Atlanta Braves for 13 seasons, formed the most prolific home run-hitting combination for one franchise:

HRs	Players	Team	Years
863	Hank Aaron (442), Eddie Mathews (421)	Braves	1954-66
859	Babe Ruth (511), Lou Gehrig (348)	Yankees	1923-34
814	Willie Mays (430), Willie McCovey (384)	Giants	1959-72
745	Duke Snider (384), Gil Hodges (361)	Dodgers	1947-61
737	Jim Rice (382), Dwight Evans (355)	Red Sox	1974-89

> " I've seen three or four perfect swings in my time. This lad has one of them. Barring a bad injury, he can go as far as he wants. "
>
> Ty Cobb, 1953

66 Jim had one of the most beautiful deliveries I've ever seen. It was almost like watching ballet. 99

RAY MILLER, 1990

PALMER'S FORMER PITCHING COACH

JIM 65 PALMER

Every Jim Palmer pitch was a poetic revelation, from the perfectly fluid motion, traditional high leg kick and effortless delivery right down to its explosive conclusion. But everything else about the big righthander was delivered with a rough edge, from his outspoken, candid and articulate views on life in general to his frustrating complaints and verbal exchanges with Baltimore manager Earl Weaver.

On the field, the strikingly handsome New Yorker was the American League's most dominating pitcher of the 1970s, a 268-game winner over a 19-season career that started with the Orioles in 1965. Off the field, he was impetuous and unpredictable, a sometimes-aloof perfectionist who frustrated Weaver, teammates and fans with a never-ending stream of mysterious ailments.

Palmer's pitching style was determined by a rotator-cuff injury that cut him down after the 1966 World Series and cost him almost two full seasons. When he returned in 1969, he had transformed from a straight power pitcher into a power/ finesse artist who could paint the corners with his still-dominant fastball, sharp-breaking curve and nasty changeup. Armed and dangerous once more, Palmer posted 20-win seasons in the nine-year stretch from 1970-78 while staking claim as the best righthander in the game.

During that run, he won three Cy Young Awards (1973, '75 and '76) and pitched in five All-Star Games. He was the ace of a powerful 1971 Orioles staff that featured a record-tying four 20-game winners. He led the Orioles to four division titles, two pennants and a World Series win (1970) while averaging 288 innings and pitching 44 of his 53 career shutouts.

Palmer, a member of three championship teams, recorded an 8-3 record in eight postseasons and 4-2 mark in six World Series, becoming the only pitcher to win fall classic games in three different decades. But success didn't stop the verbal war with Weaver, who prodded Palmer about imagined injuries. "The only thing Weaver knows about pitching is that he couldn't hit it," Palmer would quip in a typical response.

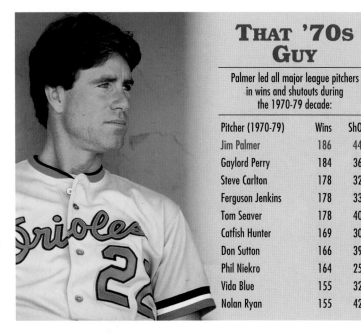

THAT '70s GUY

Palmer led all major league pitchers in wins and shutouts during the 1970-79 decade:

Pitcher (1970-79)	Wins	ShO
Jim Palmer	186	44
Gaylord Perry	184	36
Steve Carlton	178	32
Ferguson Jenkins	178	33
Tom Seaver	178	40
Catfish Hunter	169	30
Don Sutton	166	39
Phil Niekro	164	25
Vida Blue	155	32
Nolan Ryan	155	42

MICKEY 66 COCHRANE

◆ *1925-1937: ATHLETICS, TIGERS*

The first thing you noticed about Mickey Cochrane was his ears, ham-size protrusions with funny little points that had to tempt baseball's hard-core bench jockeys. The second was the respect he commanded—ears and all—as one of the grittiest and smartest leaders the game has produced. Cochrane was equal parts fascinating, contradictory and puzzling in his never-wavering dedication to—and obsession for—winning.

History remembers him as one of the best Depression-era catchers, the heart and soul of a Connie Mack Philadelphia Athletics machine that captured three straight American League pennants and consecutive World Series titles from 1929-31. Others recall the intense, driven player/manager of a Detroit team that won two straight pennants and one World Series in 1934 and '35.

Cochrane, both player and manager, was a whirling dervish, a savvy student who never stopped looking for an edge that could mean the difference between winning and losing. Nobody took defeat harder and that was reflected by the way he played, the caged-tiger manner in which he prowled the dugout and the emotional demands he made on teammates.

The man Mack credited as the driving force behind his Philadelphia champions was an agile, take-charge catcher who could change the course of games with his powerful arm or a lefthanded swing that sprayed line drives to every section of the park. Cochrane, a selective hitter who seldom struck out, topped .300 eight times en route to a .320 career average and he won two MVPs—the League award in 1928 and the baseball writers' honor six years later.

The emotional peaks and valleys took their toll on Cochrane in 1936 when, two years after winning his second MVP, he suffered a midseason nervous breakdown. The following spring, a pitch from New York's Bump Hadley beaned Cochrane, fracturing his skull in three places and prematurely ending his playing career in its 13th season. Cochrane's on-field association ended in August 1938 when he was replaced as manager.

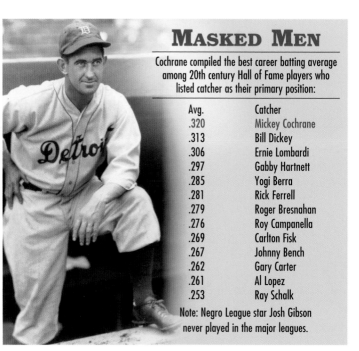

MASKED MEN

Cochrane compiled the best career batting average among 20th century Hall of Fame players who listed catcher as their primary position:

Avg.	Catcher
.320	Mickey Cochrane
.313	Bill Dickey
.306	Ernie Lombardi
.297	Gabby Hartnett
.285	Yogi Berra
.281	Rick Ferrell
.279	Roger Bresnahan
.276	Roy Campanella
.269	Carlton Fisk
.267	Johnny Bench
.262	Gary Carter
.261	Al Lopez
.253	Ray Schalk

Note: Negro League star Josh Gibson never played in the major leagues.

"He had catching intuition, a flair for outguessing the other side. Ty Cobb wearing a mask."

CONNIE MACK

COOL 67 PAPA BELL

◆ 1922-1950: NEGRO LEAGUES

No, Cool Papa Bell could not hit the wall switch and hop into bed before the light went out. And, no, he never hit a ball through the pitcher's legs and got hit by it while sliding into second base. But the point of those exaggerations should not be lost on the modern baseball fan: Bell was fast, very fast; possibly faster than any player in history.

Like fellow Negro League stars Josh Gibson, Buck Leonard and Oscar Charleston, however, Bell never got to show how fast at the major league level. But he did perform in enough barnstorming games against big-league players to make an impression. "He could run like a deer," marveled Frank Frisch. "The smoothest center fielder I've ever seen," said Paul Waner. "He'd steal the pitcher's pants," added an admiring Pie Traynor.

Bell, a stringbean 6-footer who weighed only 145 pounds, wielded his speed like a club over a two-decade-plus career that started in 1922. The switch-hitter slashed and poked balls through the infield and placed bunts as if he had the ball on a string. Legend has it Bell never batted below .308 and most of his averages were in the .350-plus range. But the real damage came after he got on base and the embellishments range from the almost-believable 175 steals in one season to two steals on one pitch.

Bell's aggressive play for such teams as the St. Louis Stars, Pittsburgh Crawfords, Kansas City Monarchs, Chicago American Giants and Homestead Grays belied the laid-back, affable personality that made him one of the most popular players on the Negro League circuit. His baserunning drew comparisons to the reckless daring of Ty Cobb, his hitting style favored Willie Keeler and his shallow-playing, go-get-'em defensive prowess reminded many of Tris Speaker.

Such lofty comparisons helped Bell gain Hall of Fame recognition in 1974—a recognition he was denied over his outstanding career as a player.

STAR POWER

When Major League Baseball staged its first All-Star Game in 1933, the American and National league teams featured 17 players who would go on to Hall of Fame distinction. When the Negro Leagues staged its first All-Star Game that same season in the same park—14 years before the modern color line would be broken—seven future Hall of Famers competed for the East and West squads, including Bell, who was the first batter in the inaugural classic:

Player	Team	Pos.
EAST		
Cool Papa Bell	Pittsburgh	CF
Oscar Charleston	Pittsburgh	1B
Josh Gibson	Pittsburgh	C
Judy Johnson	Pittsburgh	3B
WEST		
Willie Wells	Chicago	SS
Bill "Willie" Foster	Chicago	P
Turkey Stearnes	Chicago	CF

◆ SPORTING NEWS SELECTS BASEBALL'S 100 GREATEST PLAYERS ◆

66 Cool Papa was one of
the most magical players
I've ever seen. **99**

BILL VEECK

OSCAR 68 CHARLESTON

His name rolled off the tongue and his game rolled off the memory of everybody who saw him play. Oscar McKinley Charleston was considered by many the greatest all-around player in Negro League history. John McGraw, the managerial brain behind the New York Giants for more than a quarter century, disagreed. McGraw called Charleston the greatest player he had ever seen—in any league.

McGraw did not offer such praise freely. What he saw in Charleston was a five-tool star who combined the speed, savvy and baserunning meanness of Ty Cobb, the hitting and center field defense of Tris Speaker and the magnetic showmanship of Babe Ruth. One minute he was clowning for the kids and women who flocked to see him play; the next he was performing with a savage determination and obsession for winning.

Charleston even was built like Ruth—a 5-foot-11, 190-pound body with a barrel chest, sizable paunch and spindly legs. He hit for both power and average from a left-handed stance, seldom dipping under the .350 mark. He could be borderline cruel when running the bases, his spikes cutting a bloody path through anyone who stood in his way. He could be hard and unyielding in any game situation, a quick-tempered wildcat who was always ready to fight.

Charleston was at his entertaining best when playing defense, stationing himself behind second base and daring anybody to hit a ball over his head. When opportunities arose, he would turn a back flip before making a catch or take an acrobatic tumble—anything to please the crowd. That was the kind of zest Charleston brought to black baseball over a three-decade playing career that began in 1915 and touched four decades with nine different teams.

He retired as a player-manager at age 48 in 1944, three years before Jackie Robinson broke the major league color barrier. His managerial career continued until 1954, when he died suddenly of a stroke.

OVERDUE RECOGNITION

In 1976, Charleston took his place among the 17 former Negro League stars and officials who have been added to the Hall of Fame since 1971. Jackie Robinson and Larry Doby, who spent most of their careers in the major leagues after short Negro League stints, are not included on this list:

Name	Induction Year
Satchel Paige	1971
Josh Gibson	1972
Buck Leonard	1972
Monte Irvin	1973
Cool Papa Bell	1974
Judy Johnson	1975
Oscar Charleston	1976
Martin Dihigo	1977
John Henry Lloyd	1977
Rube Foster	1981
Ray Dandridge	1987
Leon Day	1995
Bill Foster	1996
Joe Rogan	1998
Joe Williams	1999
Turkey Stearnes	2000
Hilton Smith	2001

"Eddie was one of the smartest
lefthanded pitchers in baseball.
He was a master of the crossfire
delivery and that was one of his
big assets."

CONNIE MACK
THE SPORTING NEWS, 1926

EDDIE 69 PLANK

P *1901-1914, 1916-1917: ATHLETICS, BROWNS*

Watching Eddie Plank work was like watching grass grow. He was a frustrating anomaly in the fast-paced baseball world of the early 20th century. In an era of no-wasted-motion efficiency and two-hour games, Plank fought a war of attrition that helped him post 305 victories, most of them for Connie Mack-managed Philadelphia Athletics teams that won six

American League pennants from 1901-14.

The somber-looking lefthander would hitch his cap, tug at his belt, inch forward, step off the rubber, shake off signs and fidget in numerous other ways before delivering a pitch to the waiting batter. Hitters facing Plank, not familiar with such brazen delay tactics, would fume and fret before chasing an intentionally bad pitch with predictable results. Plank also talked to himself in a distinctive nasal tone that could be heard in both dugouts.

But Plank was much more than psychological gamesmanship. He also was a fierce competitor who attacked hitters with a better-than-average fastball, a good curve and uncanny control that allowed him to work to spots and make hitters chase pitches on his terms. Plank also went after lefthanded batters with a devastating crossfire

pitch—a wicked sidearm delivery that appeared to be coming from first base—and further helped his cause with a runner-freezing pickoff motion.

The strong-jawed, no-nonsense Plank, who graduated from Gettysburg College before pitching his first major league game at age 25, converted his unusual pitching style into seven 20-victory seasons for the A's and a 21-win 1915 campaign for St. Louis in the outlaw Federal League. His ERAs were consistently low, his strikeout totals high and he pitched 69 career shutouts, more than any other lefthander.

Plank also carved out an impressive 1.32 ERA over seven games and 54⅔ innings in four World Series, even though his hard-luck record was only 2-5. Plank still owns numerous pitching records in the long history of the Athletics franchise.

STRAIGHT A'S

Anybody who wonders where Plank rates in the long history of Athletics baseball needs only check out the numbers:

Category	Rank	Total
Wins	1st	284
Losses	1st	162
Innings	1st	3,860.2
ERA	3rd	2.39
Strikeouts	1st	1,985
Walks	1st	913
Games	2nd	524
Shutouts	1st	59

ALEX 70 RODRIGUEZ

<small>SS</small> *1994-PRESENT: MARINERS, RANGERS, YANKEES* <small>3B</small>

He has heard the comparisons—Ruth, DiMaggio, Aaron, Mantle, Mays—and lived with the pressure of a $252 million contract and New York pinstripes. And still the man known simply as A-Rod moves inexorably toward the greatness scouts first projected when they watched him as a 17-year-old high school phenom. Alex Rodriguez is a new-generation, five-tool prototype who has been choreographed for success.

If there's a flaw in the game of the slick and savvy third baseman, it's that he doesn't play with the on-field flair of such contemporaries as Yankees teammate Derek Jeter or Baltimore shortstop Miguel Tejada. But it's hard to argue with his near-perfect mechanics, durability, instincts and career numbers. A-Rod was the first player to hit 400 home runs before his 30th birthday, and at age 29 he already owned a batting championship, three home run titles, two Gold Gloves and distinction as the game's third 40-homer, 40-steal man.

It's easy to spot A-Rod in a baseball crowd. He's the 6-3 slugger with the DiMaggio stride and blazing bat speed who drives pitches to all fields. And he's the tall, graceful infielder with the deceptive range and powerful arm. Rodriguez spent 10 of his first 12 major league seasons as a run-producing shortstop before moving to third after being traded to the Yankees.

From 1996 (his first full year in the majors) through '99, Rodriguez and Ken Griffey Jr. combined to hit 352 home runs for the young and improving Seattle Mariners. But Griffey was traded to Cincinnati before the 2000 season, and A-Rod left Seattle the next winter when Texas offered him a whopping 10-year free-agent contract. He piled up homer totals of 52, 57 and 47 in three seasons with the Rangers and won an MVP.

In his first two pressure-filled New York campaigns, A-Rod extended his streak of 100-RBI seasons to eight and even drove in 10 runs in one game. After struggling a bit in 2004, he rebounded big in a .321, 48-homer, 130-RBI 2005 season.

A-OK

How A-Rod's 10 full seasons average out when compared with the best 10-year stretches of top players of the past and present:

Player (Years)	Avg.	R	HR	RBI
Alex Rodriguez (1996-05)	.309	123	42	121
Sammy Sosa (1995-04)	.286	105	48	123
Ken Griffey Jr. (1991-00)	.277	101	40	113
Mike Schmidt (1978-87)	.277	96	36	103
Willie Mays (1957-66)	.314	118	39	109
Hank Aaron (1957-66)	.318	113	38	117
Barry Bonds (1995-04)	.315	118	44	108

"I have incredible motivation to go out and improve every day. Integrity-wise, I cannot allow whether the team is winning or not to affect me. I'm going to give maximum effort. I have to look at myself every day and judge myself on my work ethic."

ALEX RODRIGUEZ
THE SPORTING NEWS, 2002

> "Every time Harmon comes to the plate, he is dangerous. He is as good a clutch hitter as there is in the league. I have more respect for him than anyone."

BOOG POWELL

FORMER ORIOLES SLUGGER
THE SPORTING NEWS, 1969

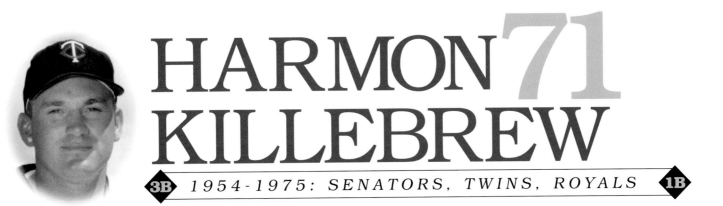

HARMON 71 KILLEBREW

3B ◆ *1954-1975: SENATORS, TWINS, ROYALS* ◆ **1B**

He was raw power, 210 pounds of muscle crammed into a 5-foot-11 frame. The thick legs supported a barrel chest and shoulders that looked like something right out of a blacksmith's shop. Harmon Killebrew was the prototypical slugger, the kind of all-or-nothing run producer who found acclaim in the power-crazy 1950s and '60s.

As a home run hitter, Killebrew was very successful. He hit 573, eighth on the all-time list, topped the 40 plateau eight times and captured six American League homer titles. A righthanded hitter with a big swing, the balding, round-faced "Killer" did not hit many line-drive home runs—most of his were towering fly balls that soared into the stands anywhere from the right-center field gap to the left field line. They usually were prodigious and memorable.

So were Killebrew's run-production numbers over 22 seasons, 21 of which were spent with a Minnesota Twins franchise that shifted from Washington in 1961. He piled up nine 100-RBI seasons en route to a career total of 1,584 and captured three RBI titles. Batting cleanup in a 1960s lineup that included Cesar Tovar, Tony Oliva, Rod Carew and Bob

Allison, Killebrew provided the hammer for offensive-minded Twins teams that lost in the 1965 World Series to Los Angeles and claimed West Division titles in 1969 and '70.

Killebrew was slow afoot and that factored into his .256 career average. He never batted higher than .288 in a full season and he never settled into a defensive position, shuttling throughout his career among first base, third and left field. But no matter where he played, he always performed solidly and without complaint.

That was typical for the gentle giant who started his career as a painfully shy rookie in 1954 and retired more than two decades later as a Minnesota icon. Killebrew, who played in 10 All-Star Games, enjoyed his signature season in 1969 when he belted 49 homers, drove in 140 runs and won MVP honors in the A.L.

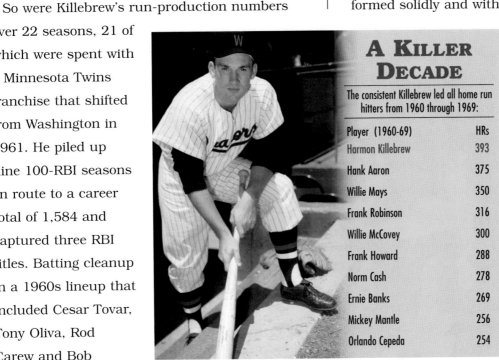

A KILLER DECADE

The consistent Killebrew led all home run hitters from 1960 through 1969:

Player (1960-69)	HRs
Harmon Killebrew	393
Hank Aaron	375
Willie Mays	350
Frank Robinson	316
Willie McCovey	300
Frank Howard	288
Norm Cash	278
Ernie Banks	269
Mickey Mantle	256
Orlando Cepeda	254

PIE 72 TRAYNOR

3B *1920-1937: PIRATES*

He was tall, rangy and broad in the shoulders, an unlikely candidate for baseball immortality. But anybody who watched Pie Traynor perform his third base magic was overpowered by the experience. Lightning-quick reflexes, long, supple arms and an unfailingly accurate throw helped him set the lofty standard by which future generations of defensive third basemen would be judged.

Traynor drew his first defensive raves when he took over as Pittsburgh's regular third baseman in 1922—his third season with the Pirates. National League players and managers had never seen anybody quite like him. Traynor would range far to his left, cutting off balls that normally skipped past overextended shortstops, or he would discourage bunters with his hard-charging gracefulness.

But he was at his best on balls hit over the bag, making lunging stops and equally acrobatic throws from awkward positions. He occasionally snared potential doubles with his bare hand, making an amazing play look easy. "Hornsby doubled down the left field line, but Traynor threw him out," was the joke that circulated through N.L. cities.

Longtime New York manager John McGraw, moved by Traynor's incredible defense against the Giants, called him the greatest team player he had ever seen. But Traynor was more than just a pretty glove. He was a dangerous righthanded hitter who compiled a .320 career average, including a 1923 season in which he batted .338 with 208 hits, 101 RBIs and 108 runs. Typically hitting fifth in Pittsburgh's lineup, Traynor topped 100 RBIs seven times while hitting only 58 career home runs.

Traynor, easy-going, friendly and articulate, often complained that his hitting was overshadowed by his fielding. But that might have been more a product of the wide-open offensive era in which he played and his lack of power. His 17-year career, which ended as a player-manager in 1937, included two visits to the World Series—the Pirates' 1925 winner over Washington and a 1927 loss to the powerful New York Yankees.

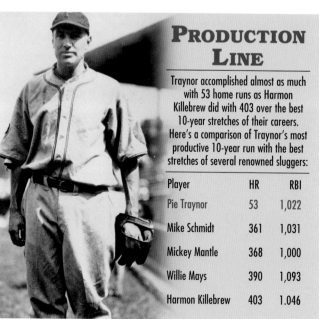

PRODUCTION LINE

Traynor accomplished almost as much with 53 home runs as Harmon Killebrew did with 403 over the best 10-year stretches of their careers. Here's a comparison of Traynor's most productive 10-year run with the best stretches of several renowned sluggers:

Player	HR	RBI
Pie Traynor	53	1,022
Mike Schmidt	361	1,031
Mickey Mantle	368	1,000
Willie Mays	390	1,093
Harmon Killebrew	403	1,046

> " If I were to pick the greatest team player in baseball today—and I have some of the greats on my own club— I would have to pick Pie Traynor. "

JOHN MCGRAW
THE SPORTING NEWS, 1929

JUAN 73 MARICHAL

P *1960-1975: GIANTS, RED SOX, DODGERS*

His leg rose up ... up ... up, until his foot was suspended over his head. Then the real run began. His leg, his right arm, his entire body swept forward in a blur and the ball swept toward home plate with unpredictable velocity and movement. Hitting against Juan Marichal was like trying to grab a fish out of a stream.

That's what it must have been like for the Philadelphia Phillies when the 22-year-old Dominican righthander made his major league debut in 1960 with a one-hit shutout. And that's what it must have been like throughout the 1960s as Marichal won 191 games, more than any other pitcher. He was the ace for a San Francisco Giants team that won one pennant and annually battled Los Angeles and St. Louis for National League superiority.

The name of Marichal's game was confidence and control. He threw five basic pitches, but never at the same speed or with the same motion. He came at hitters sidearm, three-quarters or over the top and the count was inconsequential because Marichal had an uncanny knack for painting the corner. Batters could not guess and their frustration was exacerbated by the impish grin that lit up his cheru-

bic face and the child-like playfulness that always accompanied him to the mound.

From 1963-69, a shockingly efficient seven-year stretch, Marichal had reason to grin as he posted six 20-win seasons with such records as 25-8, 25-6 and 26-9. His ERAs were equally impressive and few pitchers could match his consistency, but he never won a Cy Young while competing against such contemporaries as Sandy Koufax, Bob Gibson and Tom Seaver.

Marichal's only weakness was an emotional fire that burned just under the surface. That emotion erupted in a 1965 bat-swinging brawl during which Marichal clubbed Dodgers catcher John Roseboro and put an indelible black mark on his image. But nothing could tarnish the .631 winning percentage (243-142) and 2.89 ERA he compiled over a 16-year career that ended in 1975 at Los Angeles.

UNDER THE RADAR

Marichal, who won 27 more games than any other pitcher in the 1960s, also posted a decade-best six 20-victory seasons. He never was rewarded with a Cy Young Award:

Pitcher (1960-69)	20 Wins	Cy Youngs
Juan Marichal	6	0
Bob Gibson	4	1
Sandy Koufax	3	3
Denny McLain	3	2
Warren Spahn	3	0
Ferguson Jenkins	3	0

158

“Put your club a run ahead in the later innings and Marichal is the greatest pitcher I ever saw.”

ALVIN DARK, 1963
FORMER GIANTS MANAGER

"I'm a Ted Williams guy, but I think Yaz will go down as the best player in Red Sox history."

JOHNNY PESKY, 1979

WILLIAMS' LONGTIME TEAMMATE

CARL 74 YASTRZEMSKI

His career was filled with Hall of Fame accomplishments. But nobody had to work harder for his rewards than Carl Yastrzemski. As keeper of the left field tradition at Boston's Fenway Park for 23 seasons, Yaz climbed a steep mountain to hero status, scratching and clawing to earn the esteem that should have naturally accompanied his considerable accomplishments.

Yastrzemski's often-strained relationship with Red Sox fans could be traced to 1961, when he accepted the left field baton passed to him by Boston icon Ted Williams. The Fenway faithful were skeptical when Yaz produced, quick to boo when he didn't. The 5-foot-11 New Yorker didn't understand their reluctance to embrace a player who would claim among his career achievements 3,419 hits, 452 home runs, a Triple Crown, an American League MVP, seven Gold Gloves, 18 All-Star Game selections and three batting titles.

Unlike the more natural hitters of the 1960s and '70s, Yaz was a grinder who spent hours in the cage and studied the game with a dedication few players could match. As a lefthanded batter with an upright stance and corkscrew swing that slashed line drives to any section of the park, he was devastating in the clutch. When things were going right, Yaz was easy to live with; when they weren't, he was moody and distant. But he never stopped working—especially defensively, as protector of Fenway's Green Monster left field wall.

Yaz reached his pinnacle in 1967, when he fueled Boston's "Impossible Dream" pennant with the last Triple Crown performance in history—a .326, 44-homer, 121-RBI masterpiece that he followed with a three-homer World Series in a loss to St. Louis. He came back in 1968 with a .301 average that ranks as the lowest ever to win a batting crown. Yaz's only other World Series appearance came in 1975, when the Red Sox dropped a seven-game heart-breaker to Cincinnati.

When Yastrzemski retired in 1983 with distinction as the first A.L. player to amass 400 homers and 3,000 hits, only Baltimore's Brooks Robinson could match his 23-year stay with one team.

100 OR BUST

Yastrzemski is one of six players to record 20 or more 100-hit seasons and the first to reach that figure in each of his first 20 years:

Player	100 Hits	Yrs. Played
Pete Rose	23	24
Carl Yastrzemski	22	23
Ty Cobb	22	24
Hank Aaron	21	23
George Brett	20	21
Eddie Murray	20	21

LEFTY 75 GOMEZ

His fastballs zipped across the plate with the same accuracy his one-liners zipped across the locker room. Lefty Gomez was masterful, whether serving as court jester or pitching ace for the New York Yankees' World Series machine of the 1930s. Equal parts humorist and pitcher, "El Goofy" brought fun and personality to a sport that sometimes took itself too seriously.

Gomez was a high-kicking 6-foot-2 lefthander who joined the Yankees as a 150-pound beanpole in 1930 and never weighed more than 175. But his fastball, powered by well-developed shoulder muscles, was one of the best in the game and he mesmerized hitters with a slow curve that served as his strikeout pitch. Backed by a lineup featuring Babe Ruth, Lou Gehrig and later Joe DiMaggio, he powered his way to four 20-win seasons, including a 26-5, 2.33-ERA masterpiece in 1934.

But the Gomez legend was built around the happy-go-lucky atmosphere he brought to the field. He had a special rapport with Ruth, who kidded and prodded Gomez relentlessly about his weak hitting. The high-strung Gomez, who drove manager Joe McCarthy batty with his dugout pacing and nervous energy, was

famous for his one-line quips, locker-room pranks and goofy on-field antics, such as the anxious World Series moment in 1936 when he stepped off the mound to watch a plane fly overhead. Nothing was sacred to the quick-witted Lefty, who kept his teammates loose and relaxed when all around them was nervous and tense.

Clown and quipster, Gomez also was one of the best big-game pitchers in the business, a reputation enhanced by his 6-0 record in five World Series and 3-1 mark in five All-Star Games. Gomez's Hall of Fame career was cut short by a series of arm problems that limited him to 24 victories and fewer than 300 innings over his final four seasons. He pitched one game for Washington in 1943 before retiring with a 189-102 final record.

UNDEFEATED

Gomez, who was the winning pitcher in a record three All-Star Games, also compiled the best pitching mark in World Series play among pitchers with at least five victories:

Pitcher	Series Record	Pct.
Lefty Gomez	6-0	1.000
Jack Coombs	5-0	1.000
Herb Pennock	5-0	1.000
Bob Gibson	7-2	.778
Allie Reynolds	7-2	.778
Red Ruffing	7-2	.778
Catfish Hunter	5-3	.625
Vic Raschi	5-3	.625
Chief Bender	6-4	.600
Waite Hoyt	6-4	.600
Whitey Ford	10-8	.555
Mordecai Brown	5-4	.555
Christy Mathewson	5-5	.500

> " Gomez showed me more speed than any man I ever had caught before. He made that ball burn into my mitt. I wonder where that skinny guy gets all of his speed. "

BILL DICKEY, 1932

TSN's ALL-DECADE TEAMS

The following All-Decade Teams reflect TSN's all-stars for the 10-year periods 1900-1909, 1910-1919, 1920-1929, etc. The goal was to find the most dominant player for each position during those spans and the three best pitchers— a lefthander, a righthander and the best of the rest.

1900s

	N.L.		A.L.
1B	Frank Chance	1B	Harry Davis
2B	Johnny Evers	2B	Nap Lajoie
3B	Tommy Leach	3B	Jimmy Collins
SS	Honus Wagner	SS	Bobby Wallace
OF	Ginger Beaumont	OF	Ty Cobb
OF	Fred Clarke	OF	Sam Crawford
OF	Cy Seymour	OF	Willie Keeler
C	Roger Bresnahan	C	Ossee Schreckengost
LHP	Noodles Hahn	LHP	Eddie Plank
RHP	Christy Mathewson	RHP	Cy Young
P	Joe McGinnity	P	Ed Walsh

1930s

	N.L.		A.L.
1B	Bill Terry	1B	Lou Gehrig
2B	Frank Frisch	2B	Charley Gehringer
3B	Pepper Martin	3B	Jimmie Foxx
SS	Arky Vaughan	SS	Joe Cronin
OF	Joe Medwick	OF	Joe DiMaggio
OF	Mel Ott	OF	Goose Goslin
OF	Paul Waner	OF	Al Simmons
C	Gabby Hartnett	C	Bill Dickey
LHP	Carl Hubbell	LHP	Lefty Grove
RHP	Dizzy Dean	RHP	Red Ruffing
P	Paul Derringer	P	Lefty Gomez

1940s

	N.L.		A.L.
1B	Johnny Mize	1B	Rudy York
2B	Eddie Stanky	2B	Bobby Doerr
3B	Bob Elliott	3B	George Kell
SS	Pee Wee Reese	SS	Lou Boudreau
OF	Ralph Kiner	OF	Joe DiMaggio
OF	Stan Musial	OF	Tommy Henrich
OF	Enos Slaughter	OF	Ted Williams
C	Ernie Lombardi	C	Birdie Tebbetts
LHP	Harry Brecheen	LHP	Hal Newhouser
RHP	Rip Sewell	RHP	Bob Feller
P	Bucky Walters	P	Dizzy Trout

1970s

	N.L.		A.L.
1B	Willie Stargell	1B	George Scott
2B	Joe Morgan	2B	Rod Carew
3B	Mike Schmidt	3B	George Brett
SS	Dave Concepcion	SS	Mark Belanger
OF	Lou Brock	OF	Reggie Jackson
OF	Cesar Cedeno	OF	Jim Rice
OF	Pete Rose	OF	Carl Yastrzemski
C	Johnny Bench	C	Thurman Munson
LHP	Steve Carlton	LHP	Vida Blue
RHP	Tom Seaver	RHP	Jim Palmer
P	Don Sutton	P	Rollie Fingers

1980s

	N.L.		A.L.
1B	Keith Hernandez	1B	Eddie Murray
2B	Ryne Sandberg	2B	Lou Whitaker
3B	Mike Schmidt	3B	George Brett
SS	Ozzie Smith	SS	Cal Ripken
OF	Tony Gwynn	OF	Rickey Henderson
OF	Dale Murphy	OF	Dave Winfield
OF	Tim Raines	OF	Robin Yount
C	Gary Carter	C	Carlton Fisk
LHP	Fernando Valenzuela	LHP	Ron Guidry
RHP	Nolan Ryan	RHP	Jack Morris
P	Lee Smith	P	Roger Clemens

1910s

	N.L.		A.L.
1B	Jake Daubert	1B	Stuffy McInnis
2B	Larry Doyle	2B	Eddie Collins
3B	Heinie Zimmerman	3B	Home Run Baker
SS	Honus Wagner	SS	Buck Weaver
OF	Max Carey	OF	Ty Cobb
OF	Sherry Magee	OF	Joe Jackson
OF	Wildfire Schulte	OF	Tris Speaker
C	Chief Meyers	C	Ray Schalk
LHP	Rube Marquard	LHP	Eddie Plank
RHP	Grover Alexander	RHP	Walter Johnson
P	Christy Mathewson	P	Ed Cicotte

1920s

	N.L.		A.L.
1B	Jim Bottomley	1B	George Sisler
2B	Rogers Hornsby	2B	Eddie Collins
3B	Pie Traynor	3B	Joe Dugan
SS	Rabbit Maranville	SS	Joe Sewell
OF	Ross Youngs	OF	Harry Heilmann
OF	Zack Wheat	OF	Babe Ruth
OF	Edd Roush	OF	Al Simmons
C	Jimmie Wilson	C	Mickey Cochrane
LHP	Eppa Rixey	LHP	Herb Pennock
RHP	Burleigh Grimes	RHP	Walter Johnson
P	Dazzy Vance	P	Waite Hoyt

1950s

	N.L.		A.L.
1B	Stan Musial	1B	Mickey Vernon
2B	Jackie Robinson	2B	Nellie Fox
3B	Eddie Mathews	3B	Al Rosen
SS	Ernie Banks	SS	Harvey Kuenn
OF	Hank Aaron	OF	Larry Doby
OF	Willie Mays	OF	Mickey Mantle
OF	Duke Snider	OF	Ted Williams
C	Roy Campanella	C	Yogi Berra
LHP	Warren Spahn	LHP	Whitey Ford
RHP	Robin Roberts	RHP	Early Wynn
P	Lew Burdette	P	Bob Lemon

1960s

	N.L.		A.L.
1B	Willie McCovey	1B	Harmon Killebrew
2B	Pete Rose	2B	Bobby Richardson
3B	Ron Santo	3B	Brooks Robinson
SS	Maury Wills	SS	Luis Aparicio
OF	Hank Aaron	OF	Mickey Mantle
OF	Roberto Clemente	OF	Frank Robinson
OF	Willie Mays	OF	Carl Yastrzemski
C	Joe Torre	C	Bill Freehan
LHP	Sandy Koufax	LHP	Whitey Ford
RHP	Bob Gibson	RHP	Dean Chance
P	Juan Marichal	P	Hoyt Wilhelm

1990s

	N.L.		A.L.
1B	Jeff Bagwell	1B	Frank Thomas
2B	Craig Biggio	2B	Roberto Alomar
3B	Matt Williams	3B	Paul Molitor
SS	Barry Larkin	SS	Cal Ripken
OF	Barry Bonds	OF	Joe Carter
OF	Tony Gwynn	OF	Juan Gonzalez
OF	Sammy Sosa	OF	Ken Griffey Jr.
C	Mike Piazza	C	Ivan Rodriguez
LHP	Tom Glavine	LHP	Randy Johnson
RHP	Greg Maddux	RHP	Roger Clemens
P	John Smoltz	P	Mike Mussina

2000s

	N.L.		A.L.
1B	Albert Pujols	1B	Carlos Delgado
2B	Jeff Kent	2B	Alfonso Soriano
3B	Scott Rolen	3B	Alex Rodriguez
SS	Edgar Renteria	SS	Miguel Tejada
OF	Barry Bonds	OF	Manny Ramirez
OF	Andruw Jones	OF	Ichiro Suzuki
OF	Jim Edmonds	OF	Garret Anderson
C	Mike Piazza	C	Jorge Posada
LHP	Randy Johnson	LHP	Mark Buehrle
RHP	Roy Oswalt	RHP	Roger Clemens
P	Eric Gagne	P	Mariano Rivera

"Robby's fastball seems to get up to the plate an inviting appetizer, and then suddenly skids across the strike zone as if on a cake of ice."

RED SCHOENDIENST, 1956

ROBIN 76 ROBERTS

P *1948-1966: PHILLIES, ORIOLES, ASTROS, CUBS*

The first distressing signs came in 1956, the year Robin Roberts became a baseball mortal. The strong right arm that had produced six consecutive 20-win, 300-inning seasons couldn't deliver fastballs with quite the same gusto or control. The legs tired quicker, the once-durable 190-pound body just would not cooperate. What had started as a race for Hall of Fame glory suddenly became a struggle for survival.

It's safe to say Roberts was remarkable—perhaps as good as any pitcher over the second half century—for that six-season stretch from 1950-55: 138 wins, 1,937⅔ innings, 161 complete games in 232 starts, 24 shutouts. And the temptation to ride his powerful arm to World Series success was just too strong for a downtrodden Philadelphia Phillies franchise, which overused its prodigy in an effort to make up for 35 years of postseason frustration.

Roberts, working between starts and on short rest, helped the Whiz Kids end that jinx in 1950 with a 20-11 record and he answered all calls while piling up consecutive win totals of 21, 28, 23, 23 and 23. But the price for that work ethic would be steep and the rewards—no more World Series, 107 wins after age 30—diminishing.

The key to success was an overpowering fastball that Roberts delivered with pinpoint control from a smooth, almost-effortless motion. It was difficult for batters to time the speed of a ball that literally slid across the plate. A so-so curve was merely window dressing and a cool, calculating demeanor masked an intense competitive fire. Roberts was willing to take the mound at a moment's notice and he never gave less than 100 percent.

When he slumped to 1-10 in 1961, the Phillies severed connections with their former ace and he began a career-ending journey that would take him to Baltimore, Houston and Chicago. Depending more on guile and determination than his once-powerful fastball, Roberts carved out 52 more wins that gave him a career-ending 19-year record of 286-245. He also finished with the dubious all-time mark of 505 home runs allowed.

THE WONDER YEARS

From 1950 through 1955, no big-league pitcher could match the workhorse effort of the reliable Roberts:

Pitcher	W	L	ShO	GS	CG	IP	SO	ERA
Robin Roberts	138	78	24	232	161	1937.2	964	2.93
Bob Lemon	124	68	16	207	116	1617.1	741	3.27
Warren Spahn	118	83	20	208	133	1688.1	932	2.94
Early Wynn	118	67	19	196	106	1526.0	844	3.09
Mike Garcia	101	65	17	195	85	1471.1	720	3.14

WILLIE 77
KEELER

◆**OF** *1892-1910: NEW YORK, BROOKLYN, BALTIMORE, YANKEES, GIANTS*

He was a 5-foot-4½, 140-pound package of baseball dynamite. Light Willie Keeler's fuse and watch him run around the bases. What "Wee Willie" lacked in size and brawn he more than made up for with an explosive style that frustrated opposing pitchers and endeared him to fans of the dead-ball era.

Keeler's game was speed and he recognized the adjustments he would need to keep up with the big boys. While others tried to drive the ball into outfield gaps, Wee Willie developed a "hit 'em where they ain't" style that would make him the scourge of the National League. He choked up midway on his 29-ounce bat, leaned over the plate and drove pitchers crazy with well-placed bunts, Baltimore-chop grounders and shallow fly-ball hits. When outfielders played shallow to stop that strategy, Keeler could power a ball over their head.

Off the field, Keeler was shy, quiet and always polite, obviously embarrassed by his diminutive size. But on the field, he was an aggressive pioneer, one of baseball's first scientific hitters and a baserunning monster who used his speed like a club against distracted defenses. Not only did he steal 495 bases over 19 seasons, he combined with Baltimore teammate John McGraw to perfect the hit-and-run and other early strategies.

Keeler's best years were spent as a go-get-'em right fielder on the Orioles' pennant-winning teams of 1894, '95 and '96—seasons in which he batted .371, .377 and .386. But his masterpiece was 1897, when he batted a whopping .424 and compiled a 44-game hitting streak that stood as the major league record until Joe DiMaggio broke it in 1941. In an eight-season stretch for Baltimore and Brooklyn from 1894-1901, Keeler never fell below .339 or failed to get 200 hits.

He remained a force well into the 20th century, emerging as the first real superstar for a New York Highlanders team that would gain later fame as the Yankees. Keeler retired in 1910 with a .341 career average and 2,932 hits—all but 419 of them singles.

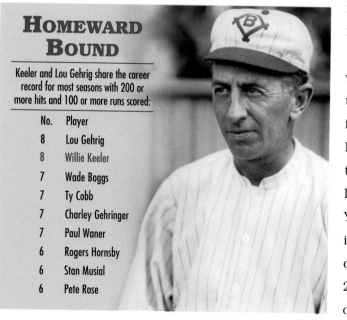

HOMEWARD BOUND

Keeler and Lou Gehrig share the career record for most seasons with 200 or more hits and 100 or more runs scored:

No.	Player
8	Lou Gehrig
8	Willie Keeler
7	Wade Boggs
7	Ty Cobb
7	Charley Gehringer
7	Paul Waner
6	Rogers Hornsby
6	Stan Musial
6	Pete Rose

"Keep your eye clear and hit 'em where they ain't."

WILLIE KEELER

WHEN ASKED HIS SECRET TO GREAT HITTING

AL 78 KALINE

He guarded the right field tradition at Tiger Stadium like a jealous lover, much as former Detroit icon Ty Cobb had done more than four decades earlier. What Al Kaline might have lacked in color and charisma he more than made up for with hard work, persistence and all-around consistency. Kaline was the battery that juiced the Tigers' attack for 22 seasons and one of the premier defensive outfielders of the 1950s and '60s.

Kaline was a graceful stylist who made the game look easy. Shy and unsmiling off the field, Kaline the player spoke volumes with an aggressive, always-heady performance that reflected an intense desire to succeed. The consistency that became a Kaline trademark was best reflected by the way he cut down runners with a strong, accurate arm and the diving, wall-banging defense that earned him 10 Gold Gloves and numerous stays on the disabled list.

Kaline, a righthanded hitter who made his big-league debut at the tender age of 18, used a feet-apart, Joe DiMaggio-like stance and lightning-quick wrists to slash line drives to all fields. He provided himself a lofty career standard in 1955 when, at age 20, he hit .340 and became the youngest batting champion in history. That early success saddled Kaline with great expectations he struggled throughout his career to fulfill, but a final .297 average, 399 home runs and 3,007 hits would suggest he more than succeeded. So would his reputation as one of the most feared clutch hitters of his era.

Despite a long list of debilitating injuries, Kaline never backed off his aggressive playing style and the fans loved him for it. They also appreciated a man who achieved career success despite a childhood operation that forced him to compete with a deformed left foot. Kaline played in 16 All-Star Games but only one World Series—a 1968 classic in which he batted .379 and helped the Tigers post a seven-game victory over the St. Louis Cardinals.

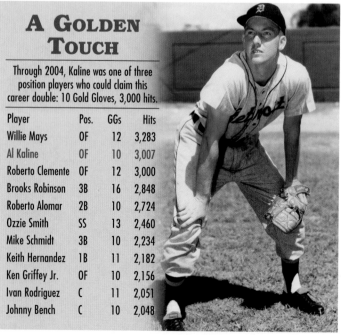

A GOLDEN TOUCH

Through 2004, Kaline was one of three position players who could claim this career double: 10 Gold Gloves, 3,000 hits.

Player	Pos.	GGs	Hits
Willie Mays	OF	12	3,283
Al Kaline	OF	10	3,007
Roberto Clemente	OF	12	3,000
Brooks Robinson	3B	16	2,848
Roberto Alomar	2B	10	2,724
Ozzie Smith	SS	13	2,460
Mike Schmidt	3B	10	2,234
Keith Hernandez	1B	11	2,182
Ken Griffey Jr.	OF	10	2,156
Ivan Rodriguez	C	11	2,051
Johnny Bench	C	10	2,048

> "I'll take Kaline over Mantle or any other young outfielder you can name. This kid is going down with the great ones of all time."

Fred Hutchinson, 1960

Former Tigers Manager

> " He loves to play. He loves to compete. And you can't compete from the dugout. "

MIKE FLANAGAN

ORIOLES PITCHING COACH
THE SPORTING NEWS, 1995

CAL 79 RIPKEN

It took him 14 grueling seasons to break Lou Gehrig's "unreachable" consecutive-games record, another three-plus to go 502 games beyond that unfathomable milestone. "The Streak" forever will be the measure of Cal Ripken Jr., but his 3,184 hits, 431 home runs, two American League MVPs and unflagging enthusiasm never will be forgotten by adoring Baltimore fans. Neither will the shot of adrenaline he gave baseball in 1995, a feel-good revitalization that lifted the game's sagging image after the fan-alienating strike of 1994.

Nobody could have envisioned Ripken as a threat to Lou Gehrig's 2,130-game streak when he broke in as an oversized shortstop in 1981. But a Rookie of the Year 1982 season, followed by a 27-homer, 102-RBI, MVP-winning 1983 campaign vaulted the quiet, no-nonsense infielder into the national consciousness and set the stage for his methodical grind toward greatness.

As a long-expected shift to third base was put off season after season, Ripken moved gracefully around his shortshop position, never flashy but making every play look easy and even winning a pair of Gold Gloves. Mr. Dependable also was a constant threat at the plate, where he changed from stance to stance but still posted power and production numbers not associated with a middle infielder. The line drive-hitting righthanded batter, who topped 20 home runs in 10 straight seasons and 100 RBIs four times, started 16 consecutive All-Star Games and combined with Eddie Murray to power the Orioles to a World Series championship in 1983.

Ripken reached his career apex on September 6, 1995, when the entire baseball world tuned in to watch him play consecutive game No. 2,131, the streak-breaker that had been the focus of an intense spotlight for several years. The night was a virtual lovefest for Baltimore's native son, who would stretch his streak to 2,632 games and his career games total to 3,001. Ironically, the man who sits atop most of Baltimore's key all-time statistical categories wound up missing 189 games over his final three seasons before retiring in 2001 as a third baseman.

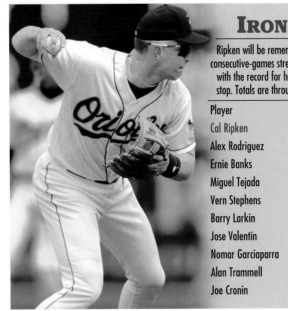

IRON BAT

Ripken will be remembered for his record consecutive-games streak, but he also retired with the record for home runs by a shortstop. Totals are through the 2005 season:

Player	HR
Cal Ripken	345
Alex Rodriguez	344
Ernie Banks	277
Miguel Tejada	216
Vern Stephens	213
Barry Larkin	194
Jose Valentin	192
Nomar Garciaparra	183
Alan Trammell	177
Joe Cronin	155

66 For my money, he's the
best player in the game
today. Other people
may disagree, but if
you're asking me what
player I'd want up there
to win a game for me,
it's Eddie Murray 99

SPARKY ANDERSON, 1986

EDDIE 80 MURRAY

1B *1977-1997: ORIOLES, DODGERS, METS, INDIANS, ANGELS*

It was easy to dismiss Eddie Murray as a secondary player in baseball's superstar cast. That's just the way the quiet, brooding first baseman wanted it. But Murray's seeming indifference couldn't mask the outstanding numbers he compiled over 21 major league seasons, and his reign as the only switch hitter (and one of four players overall) to achieve both 3,000 hits and 500 home runs probably will be a long one.

Murray, shy and distrustful, played the game with a perpetual scowl, a facade that only teammates and close friends were allowed to penetrate. But those who did discovered a warm, hard-working, no-nonsense craftsman with a disdain for the spotlight, a smooth glove and a lethal swing from either side of the plate. What the 6-2, 210-pound Los Angeles kid lacked in media-friendly charisma he more than made up for with an intense desire to succeed and his ability to perform in the clutch.

The intimidating demeanor helped Murray thrive in a "Bad Oriole, Good Oriole" combination with Baltimore shortstop Cal Ripken. While the clean-shaven Ripken won the hearts of Orioles fans with his durable consistency, Murray played the role of enforcer—an image perpetuated by his crouched, uncoiling left-handed stance. The Ripken-Murray-led Orioles won a World Series championship in 1983.

Murray, a three-time Gold Glove winner, played for Baltimore through 1988 (and returned for half a season in 1996). He made hired-gun stops with the Los Angeles Dodgers, New York Mets, Cleveland Indians and Anaheim Angels before retiring in 1997. Murray's 3,255 career hits rank No. 2 all-time among switch hitters behind Pete Rose, and only Mickey Mantle connected for more switch-hit homers than Murray's 504. Murray, who played in a major league-record 2,413 games at first base, hit home runs from both sides of the plate in the same game 11 times, another record, and he is third behind leader Lou Gehrig and Manny Ramirez on the all-time grand-slam list with 19.

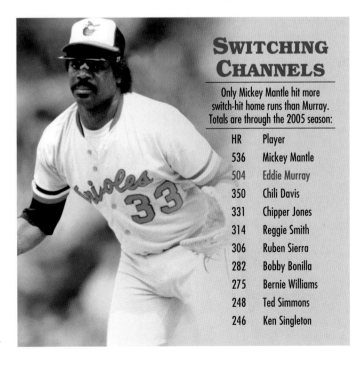

SWITCHING CHANNELS

Only Mickey Mantle hit more switch-hit home runs than Murray. Totals are through the 2005 season:

HR	Player
536	Mickey Mantle
504	Eddie Murray
350	Chili Davis
331	Chipper Jones
314	Reggie Smith
306	Ruben Sierra
282	Bobby Bonilla
275	Bernie Williams
248	Ted Simmons
246	Ken Singleton

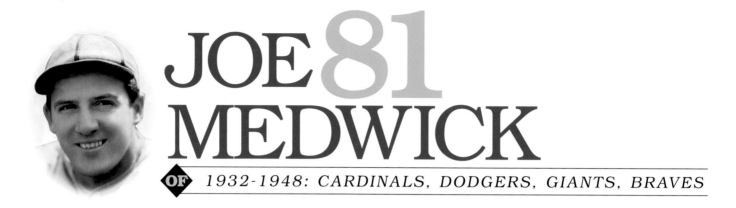

JOE 81 MEDWICK

◆ 1932-1948: CARDINALS, DODGERS, GIANTS, BRAVES

If Dizzy Dean was the heart of St. Louis' Gashouse Gang, Joe Medwick was its soul. He also was the enforcer for the colorful Cardinals who battled fate, opponents and each other during a raucous Depression-era run that produced laughs and tears, bumps and bruises and a 1934 World Series championship. What the hard-edged left fielder couldn't conquer with his lusty bat, he often challenged with his equally dangerous fists.

Medwick was a perfect fit for baseball's rugged 1930s style. Quick-tempered, he competed with an aggressive intensity that angered opponents and often befuddled his own teammates. "If you want to be a clown, join the circus," he shouted at Dean, Rip Collins, Pepper Martin and other cut-up teammates who worked him into a perpetually agitated state. Medwick released his fury with slashing line drives from a big righthanded swing that spread terror throughout the National League.

The pitch didn't have to be good; it just had to be within reach. Medwick was an offensive machine in a five-season stretch from 1935-39, piling up 1,075 hits and 657 RBIs, leading the league in doubles and RBIs three times and capturing an MVP. His .374, 31-homer, 154-RBI performance in 1937 produced the last Triple Crown in N.L. history.

"Ducky"—the nickname spoofed his duck-like walk—remained an offensive madman until 1940 when, shortly after he was traded to Brooklyn because of a salary dispute, former Cardinals teammate Bob Bowman drilled him in the head with a pitch, almost ending his career. Medwick came back to post solid numbers and helped the Dodgers win a 1941 pennant, but he never hit with the old passion.

Medwick is best remembered as the left fielder who had to be removed from the seventh game of the 1934 Series by commissioner Kenesaw Mountain Landis because he was being pelted with garbage by outraged Detroit fans. Medwick was targeted after his hard slide into Tigers third baseman Marv Owen during the Cardinals' 11-0 title-clinching win.

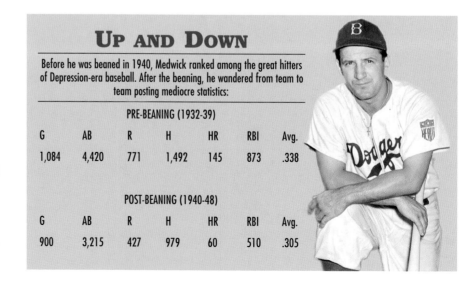

UP AND DOWN

Before he was beaned in 1940, Medwick ranked among the great hitters of Depression-era baseball. After the beaning, he wandered from team to team posting mediocre statistics:

PRE-BEANING (1932-39)

G	AB	R	H	HR	RBI	Avg.
1,084	4,420	771	1,492	145	873	.338

POST-BEANING (1940-48)

G	AB	R	H	HR	RBI	Avg.
900	3,215	427	979	60	510	.305

66 He was the meanest, roughest guy you could imagine. He just stood up there and whaled everything within reach. Doubles, triples, home runs; he sprayed 'em all over every park. 99

LEO DUROCHER, 1949

"From Kansas City to Kankakee and back again, I ain't never seen nothing like (Robinson). And then, when you see him you don't believe it."

CASEY STENGEL, 1974

BROOKS 82 ROBINSON

3B *1955-1977: ORIOLES*

The hunched shoulders and loping run made Brooks Robinson easy to spot. But it took a hot ground ball within hailing distance of third base to give him perspective. The eyes would flash, the reflexes would kick in and the glove would streak toward a white blur barely discernible to the human eye. Another accurate throw would complete another masterful play by baseball's "human vacuum cleaner."

Robinson's 23-year Baltimore legacy was built around scores of potential hits he stole from frustrated opponents. His 11 American League fielding-average titles offer testimony to the routine plays he always made and his 16 Gold Gloves reflect the tumbling, acrobatic gyrations he often pulled off with dramatic flair. Robinson, who made his Orioles debut in 1955 at age 18, was slow afoot and his arm was only average, but his reflexes and dexterity were exceptional and his quick release and throwing accuracy uncanny.

Robinson is best remembered for his defense, but the righthanded punch and even-keeled leadership he added to the powerful Orioles' lineups of the 1960s and '70s cannot be overlooked. A disciplined hitter with a team-first attitude, Robinson topped 20 home runs six times and earned an A.L. MVP in 1964 when he

batted .317 with 118 RBIs. He was especially dangerous in the clutch and his gracious, personable demeanor lifted him to icon status among adoring Baltimore fans.

The R&R combination of Brooks and Frank Robinson combined for 72 homers and 222 RBIs in 1966 and the Orioles won the first of four pennants and two World Series in a six-year span. The 1970 fall classic belonged to Brooks, who batted .429 and put on a defensive clinic, stealing hit after hit from the disbelieving Reds while claiming MVP honors.

"The guy can field a ball with a pair of pliers," Cincinnati star Pete Rose grumbled, expressing the frustration felt by Robinson contemporaries for almost a quarter century—a quarter century that produced still-standing third base fielding records for percentage, assists, putouts, chances and double plays.

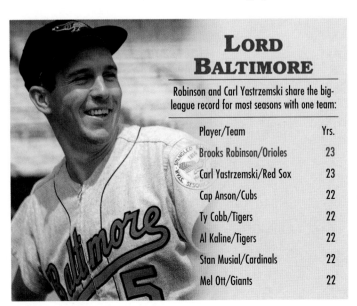

LORD BALTIMORE

Robinson and Carl Yastrzemski share the big-league record for most seasons with one team:

Player/Team	Yrs.
Brooks Robinson/Orioles	23
Carl Yastrzemski/Red Sox	23
Cap Anson/Cubs	22
Ty Cobb/Tigers	22
Al Kaline/Tigers	22
Stan Musial/Cardinals	22
Mel Ott/Giants	22

WILLIE 83 STARGELL

1B *1962-1982: PIRATES*

The towering drives that registered 7s and 8s on baseball's Richter scale provided a stark contrast to the gentle manner in which Willie Stargell practiced his craft. As a lumbering 6-foot-3, 225-pound, bat-waving slugger, Stargell could be frightening. As the easy-going leader of Pittsburgh's clubhouse, he could be inspiring. Nobody combined these seemingly divergent qualities more effectively than the man young Pirates players came to know affectionately as "Pops."

Stargell was a classic power hitter. He stood deep in the box with feet spread apart and attacked the pitch with a long, hard swing. The ball left his bat like a bazooka shot and he quickly gained a reputation for long home runs—two balls out of Dodger Stadium, seven out of Forbes Field, four into the upper deck at Three Rivers Stadium. He also hit a lot of them—National League-leading totals of 48 in 1971, 44 in 1973—while carving a niche alongside the top power hitters of the era.

In between his 475 career home runs and 1,936 strikeouts (No. 5 all-time), Stargell collected enough hits to compile a solid .282 average over a 21-year career that began in 1962. The seven-time All-Star Game performer also worked hard to become one of the more reliable defensive first basemen in the game. But the Stargell legacy is about much more than long homers and numbers.

The fun-loving, quick-to-smile slugger learned from early career mentor Roberto Clemente and evolved into one of the game's most influential team leaders. The Pirates captured the 1971 World Series with Clemente leading the charge, but the 1979 championship, fueled by Stargell's "We Are Family" approach, belonged to Pops.

First the 39-year-old Stargell was named N.L. co-MVP after a 32-homer, 82-RBI regular season. Then he earned MVP honors in an NLCS victory over Cincinnati with a .455 average and two home runs. He completed his MVP triple when he batted .400 and hit a World Series-deciding homer in Game 7 against Baltimore.

POPS IS TOPS

In the 1970-79 decade, nobody hit more home runs than the Pirates' Stargell:

Player (1970-79)	HRs
Willie Stargell	296
Reggie Jackson	292
Johnny Bench	290
Bobby Bonds	280
Lee May	270
Dave Kingman	252
Graig Nettles	252
Mike Schmidt	235
Tony Perez	226
Reggie Smith	225

"I never have seen a batter who hits the ball any harder. For sheer crash of bat meeting ball, Stargell simply is the best."

HARRY WALKER
FORMER PIRATES MANAGER
THE SPORTING NEWS, 1965

66 I don't chase Mark McGwire's
shots—I admire them. 99

STEVE FINLEY

PADRES CENTER FIELDER
THE SPORTING NEWS, 1997

MARK 84 McGWIRE

The swing was short and compact, hitting reduced to its simplest terms. The bat speed that fueled Mark McGwire's growing mystique was generated by massive shoulders and tree-trunk biceps that accentuated his 6-5, 245-pound frame. The St. Louis Cardinals first baseman presented a menacing figure as he stood in the box, slightly crouched and unflinchingly focused, and slowly swooshed his

bat back and forth across the plate with devious anticipation.

That picture became ingrained in the national consciousness during the magic summer of 1998, when McGwire led a home run parade that defied logic and shattered Roger Maris' 37-year-old single-season record. Not only did Big Mac finish with an improbable 70 homers, Chicago Cubs slugger Sammy Sosa hit 66—and finished as a footnote. McGwire followed his feel-good summer of '98 with a National League-best 65 homers, fell off to 32 in 2000 and abruptly retired after an injury-plagued, 29-homer campaign in 2001.

McGwire, whether entertaining the early-arriving masses during batting practice or locking in his radar during a game, was instant excitement. He didn't just hit the ball out of the park with quiet consistency—he hit missiles that generally registered 450 feet or more on baseball's tape

measure. He was frustratingly selective, unwavering in his commitment to waiting for the perfect pitch, and when he got it he hit the ball farther with less effort than anybody in the game.

The big redhead was uncomfortable with the Babe Ruth-like aura he was accorded. But he was an unwitting victim of his own accomplishments—49 home runs in his Rookie of the Year 1987 season with Oakland, four consecutive 50-plus homer performances with the A's and Cardinals, six 100-RBI seasons and 583 career homers. McGwire also was a solid first baseman with soft hands and surprising agility. He never reached the World Series in his four-plus St. Louis seasons, but he and bash brother Jose Canseco helped power the A's to three consecutive American League pennants and a 1989 World Series title in their five full seasons together.

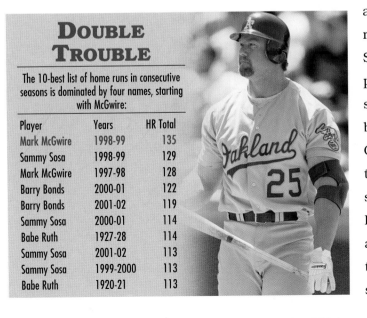

DOUBLE TROUBLE

The 10-best list of home runs in consecutive seasons is dominated by four names, starting with McGwire:

Player	Years	HR Total
Mark McGwire	1998-99	135
Sammy Sosa	1998-99	129
Mark McGwire	1997-98	128
Barry Bonds	2000-01	122
Barry Bonds	2001-02	119
Sammy Sosa	2000-01	114
Babe Ruth	1927-28	114
Sammy Sosa	2001-02	113
Sammy Sosa	1999-2000	113
Babe Ruth	1920-21	113

ED 85 WALSH

P *1904-1917: WHITE SOX, BRAVES*

He was strong, cocky and confident, qualities that served him well as one of the most prolific workhorse pitchers of the early 1900s. But a little less swagger and considerably more restraint might have prolonged Ed Walsh's fleeting moment in the spotlight and allowed him to challenge the career numbers posted by Christy Mathewson, Walter Johnson and other turn-of-the-century greats.

The 6-foot-1 Walsh was a rubber-arm righthander and king of the legal spitballers. He also was a dapper, fun-loving, happy-go-lucky charmer who approached his work with youthful exuberance and defiance. An above-average fastball and mediocre curve got him to the major leagues in 1904, but it wasn't until he unleashed his devastating spitter in 1906 that he joined the baseball elite.

That was the season he posted a 17-13 regular-season record for the Hitless Wonder White Sox and keyed a World Series victory over the powerful Cubs with two more wins in the all-Chicago classic. Buoyed by that success and a spitball that "dropped like a 10-pound brick," Walsh became a pitching machine, working scheduled starts and providing between-start relief.

The more work the better, and Walsh upped his win total to 24 in 1907 and his innings count to a whopping 422⅓. That set the stage for the most prolific season of the modern era. In a memorable 1908 campaign, Walsh compiled a 40-15 record, completed 42 of 49 starts, appeared in a league-leading 66 games and struck out 269 batters in a modern-record 464 innings. Despite his yeoman effort and 1.42 ERA, the White Sox could finish no better than third in the American League.

Walsh never reached that height again, but he did post consecutive 27-win records in 1911 and '12 while completing a 168-112 seven-year run in which he worked 2,526⅓ innings—an average of 361. Big Ed battled a tired arm for five more seasons, winning only 13 times and never again topping 100 innings. Walsh's 195-126 career mark was impressive, but his 1.82 ERA over 14 seasons is the lowest in modern history.

FIVE-YEAR PLANS

Walsh, who delivered his spitball with gripping success, ranks among baseball's pitching elite when comparing top five single-season win totals:

Total	Name/Seasons
158	Christy Mathewson (37, 33, 31, 30, 27)
149	Grover Alexander (33, 31, 30, 28, 27)
149	Walter Johnson (36, 33, 28, 27, 25)
147	Joe McGinnity (35, 31, 28, 27, 26)
140	Cy Young (33, 32, 28, 26, 21)
136	Ed Walsh (40, 27, 27, 24, 18)
134	Jack Chesbro (41, 28, 23, 21, 21)
132	Lefty Grove (31, 28, 25, 24, 24)
128	Mordecai Brown (29, 27, 26, 25, 21)
124	Bob Feller (27, 26, 25, 24, 22)

> I could make (the spitball) break four different ways—in, out, up or down. It just depended on how I delivered the ball. I'd throw eight spitballs out of every 10 pitches. A spitball is so much more effective than a curve because it breaks more sharply.

ED WALSH, 1956

DUKE 86
SNIDER

OF *1947-1964: DODGERS, METS, GIANTS*

He was the Duke of Flatbush, a Boy of Summer and a charter member of the Dem Bums fraternity that graced Brooklyn's Ebbets Field in the late 1940s and '50s. And the image of a graceful, handsome young Duke Snider patrolling center field and driving pitches onto Bedford Avenue still burns deep in the Borough of Churches.

Snider was the unofficial enforcer and most critically analyzed enigma for a franchise that dominated the National League standings through most of his career.

The prematurely gray, free-swinging Snider, a speedy lefthanded pull hitter tailored for tiny Ebbets Field, was a power source who topped 40 home runs from 1953-57 and averaged more than 100 RBIs over the same five-year stretch. He also was fast and instinctive, one of the best defensive outfielders in the game. But no matter how Snider produced, he never could fully please demanding Brooklyn fans who thought he lacked the passion of his more intense Dodgers teammates.

Part of the image problem resulted from Snider's tell-it-like-it-is bluntness and the inner rage he directed at his own failings. It also stemmed from a sensitivity fueled by constant comparisons to two contemporary New York center fielders—Mickey Mantle and Willie Mays. But it's hard to knock

Snider's .295 career average, 407 home runs and big-game efficiency—an N.L.-record 11 homers and 26 RBIs in six World Series, two of which resulted in Dodgers championships.

Snider, who appeared in seven All-Star Games, was a force through his Brooklyn career, but his hitting dropped off in 1958 when the Dodgers moved to his hometown of Los Angeles. Frustrated by the vast right-center field dimensions of the Coliseum and playing without most of his Brooklyn teammates, Snider never topped 23 home runs or 88 RBIs again before closing his career in San Francisco. Still, he remains the Dodgers franchise record-holder for home runs (389), RBIs (1,271) and extra-base hits (814).

DUKING IT OUT

Snider matched up evenly against rival New York-based center fielders Willie Mays and Mickey Mantle in the four-year period from 1954-57, when all three were in their prime:

Player	Average	HR	RBI	R	Hits
Snider	.305	165	459	449	662
Mays	.323	163	418	455	746
Mantle	.330	150	425	503	682

" I'm going to say (Snider's) the best outfielder in the major leagues today. And that includes Mickey Mantle, Stan Musial and Ted Williams. "

BEANS REARDON

LONTIME NATIONAL LEAGUE UMPIRE
THE SPORTING NEWS, 1955

> A tremendous hitter. Hardly any pitchers who pitched against (Crawford) are still alive. Half of 'em died of heart attacks.

CASEY STENGEL, 1957

SAM 87 CRAWFORD

◆ 1899-1917: REDS, TIGERS

Sam Crawford stood out like a sore thumb. The enormous shoulders, the muscular, well-conditioned body and the hard, menacing swing were futuristic illusions in a turn-of-the century era that glorified its speedy contact hitters. Wahoo Sam (he was born and raised in Wahoo, Neb.) was more typical of the sluggers who would thrive after the 1920s and his contemporaries claimed he could have

posted Babe Ruth-like home run totals if he had been born 20 years later.

So Crawford had to settle for a reputation as the hardest hitter of the dead-ball era. He stood erect in his lefthanded stance, feet spread, and whaled away at the offerings of pitchers he often intimidated. Many of his vicious line drives ended up in outfielders' gloves just short of the fence, but many others whistled into the gaps—and beyond.

Crawford, who began his career in 1899 with Cincinnati, holds distinction as the first player to lead both leagues in home runs—16 in 1901 with the Reds; seven in 1908 with the Tigers. But Crawford, who was not considered fast, is even better known for another kind of extra-base hit. He led his league six

times in triples (he had at least 10 in every full season he played) and still holds the all-time record for three-base hits with 309, 14 more than longtime Detroit teammate Ty Cobb.

Crawford and Cobb, who worked side-by-side in Detroit's outfield for 13 years, formed a formidable combination that fueled the Tigers to three straight American League pennants from 1907-09. But Crawford, the cleanup man, was overshadowed for most of his career by the fiery Cobb, who in turn resented Crawford's emotional connection with the fans of Detroit.

Still they performed well in tandem, Cobb as the instigator and Crawford as one of the most dangerous clutch hitters in the game, until 1917 when Crawford ended his 19-year career with a .309 average.

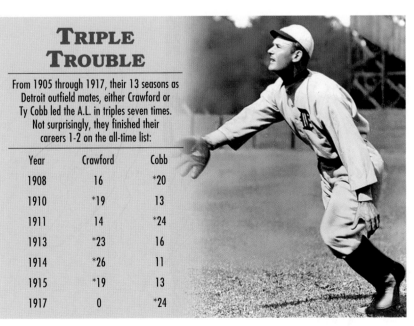

TRIPLE TROUBLE

From 1905 through 1917, their 13 seasons as Detroit outfield mates, either Crawford or Ty Cobb led the A.L. in triples seven times. Not surprisingly, they finished their careers 1-2 on the all-time list:

Year	Crawford	Cobb
1908	16	*20
1910	*19	13
1911	14	*24
1913	*23	16
1914	*26	11
1915	*19	13
1917	0	*24

DIZZY 88 DEAN

P *1930-1941, 1947: CARDINALS, CUBS, BROWNS*

He was the lovable, colorful, cornpone-spewing righthander who helped fuel the success of St. Louis' Gashouse Gang in the Depression-wracked 1930s. Dizzy Dean had the stuff of which legends are made, whether dazzling National League hitters with his powerful arm or sportswriters, teammates and fans with his braggadocio and glib tongue.

Dean's supreme confidence could be annoying, but he backed up his boasts in a short-but-sweet career that ended all too prematurely because of an arm injury.

Ol' Diz, the self-ascribed moniker that reflected his poor Arkansas roots, was a baseball character. But he also was a 6-foot-2, strong-armed strikeout pitcher with a blazing fastball, a good curve and a nasty changeup. The

BROTHERLY LOVE

When Dizzy and Paul Dean combined for 49 wins in 1934, they set a single-season record no brother combination has been able to match. Here are the best seasons for the top brother duos through 2005:

Year	Brothers/Wins	Total
1934	Dean, Dizzy (30), Paul (19)	49
1970	Perry, Jim (24), Gaylord (23)	47
1979	Niekro, Phil (21), Joe (21)	42
1916	Coveleski, Harry (21), Stan (15)	36
1924	Barnes, Virgil (16), Jesse (15)	31
1995	Martinez, Ramon (17), Pedro (14)	31
1982	Forsch, Bob (15), Ken (13)	28
1977	Reuschel, Rick (20), Paul (5)	25
1907	Mathewson, Christy (24), Henry (0)	24
1988	Perez, Melido (12), Pascual (12)	24
1995	Maddux, Greg (19), Mike (5)	24

> "Going anywhere with (Dizzy) was like going with a brass band. He had a great sense of humor and was just a very interesting character."
>
> PHIL WRIGLEY
> THE SPORTING NEWS, 1974

always-smiling Dean fired his pitches with the same fluid delivery with which he fired barbs at hitters who let the good-natured ribbing add to their frustration.

Dean was the class of the N.L. from 1932, his first full big-league season, through 1936, a five-year stretch in which he won 120 games and led the league in strikeouts four times. He was a magnificent 30-7 in an MVP 1934 season in which he combined with brother Paul, a 19-game winner, to lead the Cardinals to a pennant and World Series victory over Detroit. The "Me 'n' Paul" Dean combination won four games in the

World Series and Dizzy remained baseball's last 30-game winner for 34 years.

Dean, who added 28 wins in 1935 and 24 more in '36, saw his career turn dramatically in the 1937 All-Star Game when he was hit on the foot by an Earl Averill line drive. Trying to pitch with a broken toe, Dean altered his delivery and suffered an arm injury that limited him to 29 wins over his final six major league seasons—five with the Chicago Cubs and one with the St. Louis Browns.

Out of work at age 31, Dean went on to wow a second generation of fans with the distinctive, fractured rhetoric he unleashed from the broadcast booth as a colorful baseball analyst.

OZZIE 89 SMITH

1978-1996: PADRES, CARDINALS

The "Oz-zie! Oz-zie!" chants started the instant he raced to his shortstop position at St. Louis' Busch Stadium. They intensified when Ozzie Smith performed his trademark back flip, an occasional embellishment he really didn't need to earn his daily ovations. The simple thought of another sensational play was enough to electrify Cardinals fans, who have a history of tender relationships with the superstars they embrace.

Smith certainly qualified for that status. Supporters claim he was the best defensive shortstop in history; critics argue he was only one of the best. Suffice to say few games were played without the Wizard of Oz flashing the acrobatic quickness that generated oohs and aahs usually reserved for offensive feats.

Smith, who won 13 Gold Gloves, was the master at throwing on the run, whether racing behind second base or deep into the hole. He also had an uncanny knack for snaring balls with a dive, scrambling to his knees and throwing out startled runners. His range was incredible and his so-so arm was amazingly accurate.

So was the contact stroke Smith worked exhaustively to perfect from either side of the plate. A low-.200 batter in his first four seasons in San Diego, he raised his average consistently after a 1982 trade to St. Louis and finished his career as a consistent .280 threat—with 2,460 hits. Smith's ability to handle the bat and run the bases (580 career steals) enabled him to hit in the No. 2 slot and play a vital role in "Whitey Ball"—the speed game favored by Cardinals manager Whitey Herzog through most of the 1980s.

A big part of Smith's game was image, and he was as articulate in the locker room as he was with the glove. A dapper dresser with a ready smile and soft-spoken charm, Smith also was a leader on Cardinals teams that won four division titles, three National League pennants and one World Series before he retired after the 1996 season. Smith hit 28 career home runs—two for each of the 14 All-Star Games in which he appeared.

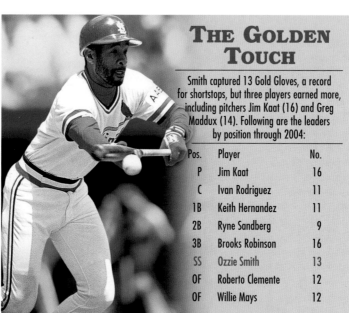

THE GOLDEN TOUCH

Smith captured 13 Gold Gloves, a record for shortstops, but three players earned more, including pitchers Jim Kaat (16) and Greg Maddux (14). Following are the leaders by position through 2004:

Pos.	Player	No.
P	Jim Kaat	16
C	Ivan Rodriguez	11
1B	Keith Hernandez	11
2B	Ryne Sandberg	9
3B	Brooks Robinson	16
SS	Ozzie Smith	13
OF	Roberto Clemente	12
OF	Willie Mays	12

> So many times I'll see the ball leave the bat and say, 'OK. That's a base hit.' And then somehow Ozzie will come up with it. A lot of the time I feel like standing out there and applauding with the rest of the fans. He's head and shoulders above every other shortstop. "

TOMMY HERR, 1987

CARDINALS SECOND BASEMAN

"Maybe there never was and never will be a perfect ballplayer. But let me ask you this: What was there Frank Frisch couldn't do?"

JOE MCCARTHY, 1962

FRANK FRISCH 90

2B *1919-1937: GIANTS, CARDINALS*

He was the heart of the New York Giants' 1920s pennant-winning machine and the soul of St. Louis' Gashouse Gang in the 1930s. Frank Frisch was addicted to winning, a craving he filled with eight World Series appearances. As a hard-nosed second baseman and one of baseball's original switch-hitters, he was a throwback to the intense, aggressive, daring, reckless style of baseball practiced at the turn of the century.

The stocky, strong-armed Frisch, a speedy four-sport star at Fordham University, never played a minor league game before stepping into a Giants lineup that produced four consecutive National League pennants—and two World Series championships—from 1921-24. Frisch brought leadership to the field, whether knocking down hot grounders with his thick chest, diving in the dirt for balls hopelessly out of reach, running the bases with flawless instinct or baiting umpires and opponents with a razor-edged tongue.

Hitting from his natural left side, Frisch, his bat wagging, was aggressive and unpredictable. He was equally capable of dragging a bunt, punching an outside pitch to left field or driving a bases-loaded double into the gap. From the right side, Frisch had more power but was less aggressive. He seldom struck out (272 times in 19 seasons) and was dangerous in the clutch—a three-time 100-RBI contributor.

Frisch was center stage in the shocking 1926 trade that sent him to St. Louis for Rogers Hornsby, the best hitter in the game. It took awhile, but Frisch overcame fan resentment over the departure of the popular Hornsby and became the leader of Cardinals teams that won pennants in 1928 and '30 and the player/manager of colorful Cardinals crews that won World Series in 1931 and '34.

Frisch, a 13-time .300 hitter who posted a .316 career average, 2,880 hits and 419 stolen bases, was the first winner of the N.L. MVP award presented by the Baseball Writers' Association of America in 1931.

SERIES BUSINESS

Through 2004, former Giants and Cardinals star Frisch ranks first among non-Yankees in six World Series categories and among the top 5 in four others:

First		Top 5	
Category	No.	Category	No.
Series	8	Triples	3
Games	50	Total bases	74
At-bats	197	Extra-base hits	13
Hits	58	Stolen bases	9
Singles	45		
Doubles	10		

RALPH 91 KINER

The full, lusty swing told you everything you needed to know about Ralph Kiner's intentions. Hit the ball hard and trot slowly around the bases before it touched asphalt or concrete. Kiner was a 6-foot-2, 195-pound baseball enforcer who brought the home run back into vogue during a short-but-productive 10-year career in the late 1940s and early 1950s.

Everything about Kiner suggested power. The broad shoulders, the fullback-like arms and legs, the quick wrists that compensated for his big swing. Long-suffering Pittsburgh fans embraced their young slugger and Kiner reciprocated, enhancing his fearsome image with torrid home run binges that left opponents shaking their heads. Five in two games. Six in three games. Four in a doubleheader. And, incredibly, eight in one four-game stretch of unrelenting destruction.

The image of a smiling, wavy-haired Kiner spread quickly through National League cities as he either won or shared home run titles in each of his first seven seasons. Twice he topped the 50 plateau and in five of those campaigns he topped 100 RBIs. And thanks to the early career tutoring of Hank Greenberg, Kiner never topped 100 strikeouts after his 1946 rookie season.

Greenberg's influence, however, could not help Kiner's suspect left field defense, improve the speed of one of baseball's slowest runners or ease the pain of playing for one of the game's weakest teams. But Kiner more than made up for those deficiencies with his intelligent, low-key, one-of-the-guys personality and amazingly consistent run production.

Kiner's final .279 average was respectable and his total of 369 home runs (36.9 per season) could have been considerably higher if not for the three prime seasons he missed during World War II and the back problems that forced a premature retirement at the still-productive age of 33. Kiner, who played in five All-Star Games, went on to a longer and on-going baseball career in the broadcast booth for the New York Mets.

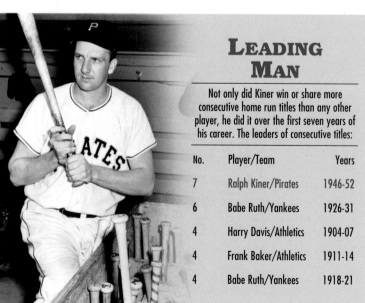

LEADING MAN

Not only did Kiner win or share more consecutive home run titles than any other player, he did it over the first seven years of his career. The leaders of consecutive titles:

No.	Player/Team	Years
7	Ralph Kiner/Pirates	1946-52
6	Babe Ruth/Yankees	1926-31
4	Harry Davis/Athletics	1904-07
4	Frank Baker/Athletics	1911-14
4	Babe Ruth/Yankees	1918-21

" I try to hit the ball as hard as
I can every time I swing. "

RALPH KINER, 1949

CHUCK 92
KLEIN

OF *1928-1944: PHILLIES, CUBS, PIRATES*

He clawed his way from an Indianapolis steel mill to the top of the baseball world. Over a five-year stretch with the Depression-era Philadelphia Phillies, Chuck Klein was as good as it gets. He belted, bashed and even threw his way into the record books with a consistency that earned him comparisons to Babe Ruth. Then, just as suddenly as he had risen, Klein faded out of the spotlight he had worked so hard to claim.

To get perspective on Klein, you start with the broad-shouldered, deep-chested, 6-foot body that was supported by relatively thin legs. It was all muscle, especially the powerful forearms that swung a 42-ounce bat from the left side like a toothpick. Klein had home run power, but fans were more likely to see his vicious drives bouncing into the gaps or off the 30-foot right field wall at tiny, hitter-friendly Baker Bowl.

The quiet, sometimes-withdrawn Klein jumped into the spotlight with a .356, 43-home run, 145-RBI effort in 1929 and through 1933 he never batted lower than .337 or posted fewer than 200 hits, 28 homers or 120 RBIs. His 1932 MVP performance was a warmup for the .368, 28-homer, 120-RBI Triple Crown he won a year later. He even set a still-standing 20th century defensive record in 1930 when he recorded 44 assists from his right field position.

But the numbers dropped sharply in 1934 when Klein was sent to Chicago by the financially strapped Phillies and he never rediscovered the stroke over an 11-season finish that took him back to Philadelphia, to Pittsburgh and back to Philly. He did have his moments, such as a 1935 World Series appearance with the Cubs and an electrifying four-home run explosion while playing for the Phillies in a game against Pittsburgh in 1936.

Klein, a National League starter in baseball's first All-Star Game in 1933, finished his Hall of Fame career in 1944 with a .320 average, 300 home runs and 2,076 hits.

No Depression

Klein's lusty hitting from 1929-33, his first five full major league seasons, averaged out nicely against the other top sluggers of the same period:

Player	H	R	HR	RBI	Avg.
Chuck Klein	224	132	36	139	.359
Jimmie Foxx	188	124	41	145	.341
Lou Gehrig	201	142	38	155	.341
Babe Ruth	170	127	43	142	.345
Al Simmons	208	120	28	144	.355

◆ SPORTING NEWS SELECTS BASEBALL'S 100 GREATEST PLAYERS ◆

"I'm not a second Babe Ruth and I don't claim to be. I don't claim that I can hit the ball as hard as Ruth."

CHUCK KLEIN, 1930

KEN 93
GRIFFEY JR.

OF *1989-PRESENT: MARINERS, REDS*

At first, he was known simply as "Junior," the kid with a mouth-watering left-handed swing and effervescent smile that lit up American League ballparks. Now, the smile is tinged with frustration, belying career numbers that portray a multi-dimensional superstar who can kill opponents softly with his glove or ravage them violently with his bat. Ken Griffey Jr. is a baseball enigma—a player whose spectacular accomplishments have been overshadowed by oversized expectations.

From Day 1 in 1989, as Seattle's 19-year-old center fielder, Griffey worked on the fringes of Jordanesque popularity. People everywhere stopped what they were doing to watch the batting practice swings of baseball's newest prodigy, and fans fell victim to his boyish charm and enthusiasm. The personality translated well to the field, where the 6-3, 205-pounder began a Ruthian drive toward greatness. Fans marveled at the effortless, short-striding, slightly uppercut swing and quick hips that allowed him to keep his hands back and hit high-floating drives into the right field stands.

Griffey, the son of Ken Griffey Sr., the right fielder for Cincinnati's Big Red Machine of the 1970s, didn't disappoint hungry Mariners fans. He consistently topped .300 and hit 398 home runs over his 11-year stay, including 56-homer seasons in 1997 and '98. The Triple Crown many predicted never materialized, but Griffey wowed fans with home runs in a record-tying eight consecutive games in 1993, a 1997 MVP award and 10 Gold Gloves—every Seattle season after his rookie year. The once-lowly Mariners, with Griffey, Alex Rodriguez and Randy Johnson leading the charge, even won A.L. West Division titles in 1995 and '97.

Griffey's post-Seattle career has not been so fruitful. Traded to Cincinnati in 2000, he hit 40 homers and topped 100 RBIs for an eighth time. But he spent much of his next four seasons on the disabled list before rebounding strongly in a healthier 2005. At age 34 in 2004, Griffey finally reached the 500-homer plateau—an extraordinary feat for most but well below the timetable that had been choreographed for "The Natural."

DIFFERENT STROKES

Griffey is one of six major leaguers to hit 40 or more home runs for different teams in consecutive seasons:

Player	Years	HRs	Teams
Andres Galarraga	1997-98	41/44	Rockies/Braves
Rafael Palmeiro	1998-99	43/47	Orioles/Rangers
Greg Vaughn	1998-99	50/45	Padres/Reds
Ken Griffey	1999-2000	48/40	Mariners/Reds
Alex Rodriguez	2000-01	41/52	Mariners/Rangers
Jim Thome	2002-03	52/47	Indians/Phillies

"Every mistake I throw. (Griffey) hits a home run. That doesn't seem fair. He can at least mix in a double every once in a while."

DAVID CONE
THE SPORTING NEWS, 1998

WADE 94 BOGGS

H is eyes locked into every pitch with laser-like precision and his mind and body reacted instinctively. To swing or not to swing never really was a question for Wade Boggs. The precise, instantaneous analysis, unwavering patience and perfect hand-eye coordination he brought to every at-bat were textbook, and the .328 average he posted over 18 major league seasons ranks among the best of all-time.

Boggs, a classic singles and doubles hitter who seldom struck out, approached his craft with machine-like consistency. He crouched slightly in his lefthanded stance, foot slightly closed, and wiggled the bat over the plate, ready to pounce. His hitting zone was sacred and nothing that penetrated it went unchallenged. But anything out of the strike zone—no matter how slightly—was off limits. During his prime with the Boston Red Sox, Boggs had the ability to foul off ball after ball until he got what he wanted, and his line drives shot to all fields—from any pitch location.

One of the best two-strike hitters ever, the 6-2 third baseman dominated the American League charts from his 1982 rookie season (after six years in the minors) through 1989, an eight-season stretch in which he won five batting titles, reached 200 hits seven straight times, led the league in doubles twice, drew more than 100 walks four times and helped the Red Sox to the 1986 World Series. Through '89, Boggs boasted a lofty .352 career average; through 1992, when his Boston days ended, he was a .338 hitter.

The sometimes-aloof, always-intense and

> **❝** He's a truly amazing hitter. He rarely swings at bad pitches, he's very selective, he gets good pitches to hit and nine times out of 10, he hits it hard. He's unbelievable, he really is. **❞**
>
> **TONY GWYNN**
> THE SPORTING NEWS, 1989

highly superstitious Boggs made a free-agent jump to the New York Yankees after the '92 season and became a two-time Gold Glove winner, although his batting average fell into slow decline. Red Sox fans cringed in 1996 as the 12-time All-Star helped the Yankees capture a World Series championship. Boggs, who was from Tampa, secured the last 210 of his 3,010 career hits as a member of the expansion Devil Rays, for whom he played in 1998 and 1999.

THE SEVEN-YEAR STRETCH

Since 1900, Boggs is the only player to collect 200-plus hits in seven consecutive years. Only two players can top his seven-season hit total in their best seven-year stretch:

Total	Player	Years
1,516	*George Sisler	1920-27
1,487	Bill Terry	1929-35
1,479	Wade Boggs	1983-89
1,463	Rogers Hornsby	1920-26
1,463	Paul Waner	1927-33
1,454	Ty Cobb	1907-13
1,450	Pete Rose	1973-79
1,448	Kirby Puckett	1986-92
1,446	Sam Rice	1924-30
1,440	Lou Gehrig	1927-33

* Sisler sat out the 1923 season with an eye problem.

SAMMY SOSA 95

OF *1989-PRESENT: RANGERS, WHITE SOX, CUBS, ORIOLES*

The home run hop and heart-tapping kiss are Sammy Sosa staples. So is the fan-melting smile that lit up Wrigley Field for 13 impressive seasons. Flamboyant, prodigious, unpredictable and always controversial, Slammin' Sammy treated Chicago to a five-year fireworks display while writing a home run legacy that only a few elite sluggers can approach.

From his 1989 debut as a 165-pound outfielder for the Texas Rangers to his glory years as a muscular, 210-pound homer machine, Sosa confounded pitchers with his productive bat and managers with his unpredictable behavior. Sosa's transformation began in 1993, his second year with the Cubs after a trade from the White Sox, when he hit 33 home runs, and it reached its peak in 2001 when he became the first player to reach the 60-homer plateau three times. His total of 292 homers over five consecutive seasons—from 1998 through 2002—might never be equaled.

His penchant for being overshadowed might not be matched, either. Sosa captured the hearts of Chicagoans when he pushed St. Louis slugger Mark McGwire in the great home run race of 1998, but McGwire set a single-season record with 70 and Sosa, with 66, settled for the consolation prize—a National League MVP award. When Sosa hit 63 homers the next season, McGwire hit 65. In Sosa's 64-homer season of 2001, San Francisco's Barry Bonds hit a record 73.

The slugging Dominican did win home run titles in 2000 (50) and 2002 (49) and his RBI totals of 158 in 1998 and 160 in 2001 were the highest in the N.L. since another Cubs star, Hack Wilson, drove in a major league-record 191 in 1930. Sosa also hit .300 or better four times and played competently, if not spectacularly, in right field for teams that generally struggled, reaching the playoffs two times.

A 2003 corked-bat suspension, several spats with managers and diminishing power numbers prompted a trade to Baltimore, but he departed as the Cubs' franchise home run leader (545) and a threat to join the elite "600 club." Sosa finished the 2005 season with 588 homers, fifth on the all-time list.

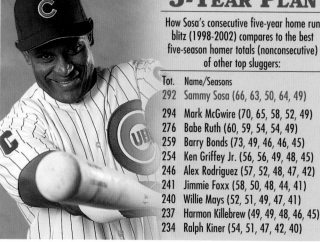

5-YEAR PLAN

How Sosa's consecutive five-year home run blitz (1998-2002) compares to the best five-season homer totals (nonconsecutive) of other top sluggers:

Tot.	Name/Seasons
292	Sammy Sosa (66, 63, 50, 64, 49)
294	Mark McGwire (70, 65, 58, 52, 49)
276	Babe Ruth (60, 59, 54, 54, 49)
259	Barry Bonds (73, 49, 46, 46, 45)
254	Ken Griffey Jr. (56, 56, 49, 48, 45)
246	Alex Rodriguez (57, 52, 48, 47, 42)
241	Jimmie Foxx (58, 50, 48, 44, 41)
240	Willie Mays (52, 51, 49, 47, 41)
237	Harmon Killebrew (49, 49, 48, 46, 45)
234	Ralph Kiner (54, 51, 47, 42, 40)

> " When he's in a hot streak, I've never
> seen a more dangerous player in my
> life, including Bonds. It doesn't matter
> who's throwing, its going to be a home
> run. It's just a matter of which pitch. "
>
> MARK GRACE
>
> FORMER CUBS TEAMMATE
> THE SPORTING NEWS, 2002

DAVE 96 WINFIELD

OF *1973-1995: PADRES, YANKEES, ANGELS, BLUE JAYS, TWINS, INDIANS*

The gap-toothed smile and soft, easy-listening voice created a false sense of security. Then Dave Winfield stood up, all 6-feet, 6-inches of him, and began swinging a bat that looked like a toothpick in his massive hands. The tall, lean body, with broad shoulders anchoring long arms, was enough to intimidate any pitcher with hopes of living through another day.

But Winfield was more than just another burly home run hitter. He was an athlete—a superior athlete—who could run, hit, throw and perform just about any other baseball skill imaginable. A college athlete at Minnesota who was drafted in three professional sports, Winfield covered plenty of ground with his long, loping stride as a left or right fielder and ended rallies with his powerful arm. He was an instinctive baserunner who got plenty of practice because of his ability to put bat on ball.

Winfield's big righthanded swing produced 3,110 hits, 465 home runs and 1,833 RBIs over a 22-year career, most of which was divided between San Diego and New York. He was a run-producer extraordinaire, first over an eight-season stint for weak Padres teams (1973-80), then for Yankees teams that benefited from a consistent string of 25-homer, 100-RBI performances.

From 1981 through '88, Winfield was a model of consistency, winning five of his seven Gold Gloves and fueling the Yankees with six 100-RBI efforts. He continued to produce while feuding publicly with owner George Steinbrenner about contracts, performance and personal matters. The image-conscious Winfield kept his cool through difficult times and maintained a delicate balance between his professional life and off-field charity work.

At least part of Steinbrenner's dissatisfaction stemmed from Winfield's less-than sterling performance and .045 average in a 1981 World Series loss to Los Angeles. But Winfield earned personal redemption 11 years later when he supplied the Series-deciding hit for Toronto in Game 6 of the 1992 fall classic. The 12-time All-Star retired in 1995, after short stints with California, Toronto, Minnesota and Cleveland.

EXCLUSIVE CLUBS

Winfield holds membership in two exclusive fraternities: He's one of three players to collect 3,000 hits, 450 homers and 200 stolen bases in his career, and he's one of three to play in 1,000 games in both the American League and National League:

HITS, HOMERS, STEALS

Player	Hits	HR	SB
Hank Aaron	3,771	755	240
Willie Mays	3,283	660	338
Dave Winfield	3,110	465	223

1,000 AND 1,000

Player	Games N.L.	Games A.L.	Total
Bob Boone	1,125	1,139	2,264
Frank Robinson	1,605	1,203	2,808
Dave Winfield	1,117	1,856	2,973

" Year after year, (Winfield) goes out there, drives in his 100 runs, never fails to hustle in every phase of the game and beats you every way a player can. "

SPARKY ANDERSON
THE SPORTING NEWS, 1988

DEREK JETER 97

He is the centerpiece of baseball's proudest franchise, a hard-nosed and savvy competitor who has earned his pinstripes with blood, sweat and tears. The blood of a warrior who dives head-first into the stands while chasing a foul pop; the sweat that comes with pressure-filled playoff games; the tears of joy shed during championship celebrations.

Derek Jeter is the inspirational leader of the New York Yankees, a role previously filled by the likes of Gehrig, DiMaggio, Mantle and Munson.

Jeter is the prototypical new-age shortstop, a graceful gloveman with a dangerous bat. But his greatest strength is the total package and winning attitude he brings to the field. Few stars can match the poise, patience and instincts Jeter uses to dissect opponents—his ability (and willingness) to steal a timely base, drop a crucial sacrifice bunt, make an intuitive defensive play and hit a key home run.

The 6-3, 195-pound Jeter is most celebrated for his intangibles, but pitchers can't ignore the dangerous inside-out swing he uses to drive the ball with deceptive power. He reached the 1,000-hit plateau by the end of his fifth full season, and in 2002 he became the only player since 1950 to score 100 runs in each of his first seven full seasons. Jeter's .314 career average ranks among the all-time Yankee greats. His resume also includes three straight 200-hit seasons, but all those numbers pale in comparison to his postseason contributions.

The new Mr. October anchored four World Series championship teams in his first five years and he ranks No. 1 all-time in postseason hits (135). New Yorkers still marvel at a heady play the six-time All-Star selection made in Game 3 of the 2001 Division Series against Oakland when he hustled to the first base side of the field to grab an errant cutoff throw and gun down the potential tying run at the plate, saving a 1-0 victory. The fluid, ever-cool Jeter—the Yankees' 11th team captain—won his first Gold Glove in 2004.

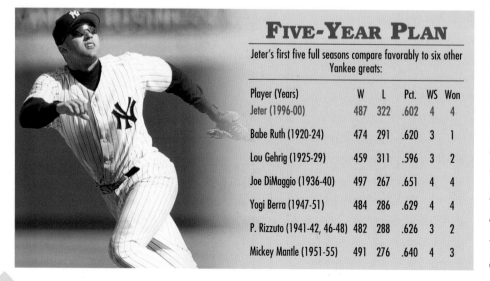

FIVE-YEAR PLAN

Jeter's first five full seasons compare favorably to six other Yankee greats:

Player (Years)	W	L	Pct.	WS	Won
Jeter (1996-00)	487	322	.602	4	4
Babe Ruth (1920-24)	474	291	.620	3	1
Lou Gehrig (1925-29)	459	311	.596	3	2
Joe DiMaggio (1936-40)	497	267	.651	4	4
Yogi Berra (1947-51)	484	286	.629	4	4
P. Rizzuto (1941-42, 46-48)	482	288	.626	3	2
Mickey Mantle (1951-55)	491	276	.640	4	3

> "There's no question his presence in the dugout is important. He's never any different, whether 4-for-4 or 0-for-4. He's still that focused, leader-type of guy."
>
> JOE TORRE
>
> YANKEES MANAGER
> THE SPORTING NEWS, 2001

GAYLORD 98
PERRY

P *1962-1983: GIANTS, INDIANS, RANGERS, PADRES, YANKEES, BRAVES, MARINERS, ROYALS*

H e was a sleight-of-hand magician, an illusionist who misdirected the concentration of batters, managers and umpires. Gaylord Perry not only loaded up pitches with foreign substances banned by baseball rules, he loaded up the thoughts of opponents with distracting mind games. He was a 314-game winner whose success can be attributed as much to guile and intelligence as to a strong arm.

After Perry's 1983 retirement, he traced the origin of his notorious spitball to 1964, his third big-league season with the San Francisco Giants. Throughout the remainder of a 22-year career that featured stops in eight cities, he was cursed by hitters, screamed at by managers and undressed by umpires searching for evidence. The laconic, broad-shouldered North Carolinian simply accepted the flareups with his best good-old-boy smile, knowing the distractions were giving him a huge psychological edge.

Before every pitch, Perry would touch various parts of his anatomy—behind the ear, his forehead, his hair, the bill of his cap, his pants leg, his wrist—as hitters waited for the dreaded spitter, a pitch that approached the plate like a fastball and dropped abruptly. More often they got Perry's above-average fastball or slider, which cut through the strike zone like daggers. The 6-foot-4 righthander converted that psychological edge into five 20-win seasons over an amazingly durable career in which he topped 250

innings 12 times.

Perry, the first pitcher to earn Cy Young Awards in both leagues, won his first in 1972 when he recorded a 24-16 record and 1.92 ERA for Cleveland. The second came in 1978 at age 40, when he finished 21-6 for San Diego. Perry was 21-13 for Cleveland in 1974, the same season brother Jim, a 215-game big-league winner, also won 17 games for the Indians.

A five-time All-Star Game performer who recorded 3,534 strikeouts, Perry never pitched in a World Series and made only one postseason appearance. That came in 1971 when he was 1-1 for the Giants in a National League Championship Series loss to Pittsburgh.

THREE-TIMERS

Perry is one of three pitchers to record their milestone 100th, 200th and 300th wins for different teams:

Pitcher	100th	200th	300th
Gaylord Perry	Giants, 1970	Indians, 1975	Mariners, 1982
Nolan Ryan	Angels, 1975	Astros, 1982	Rangers, 1990
Roger Clemens	Red Sox, 1990	Blue Jays, 1997	Yankees, 2003

> "Eck always throws strikes and he has the heart of a giant. His natural response is to challenge a crisis head-on. That's what makes him such a great reliever."

DAVE DUNCAN, 1988

ECKERSLEY'S LONGTIME PITCHING COACH

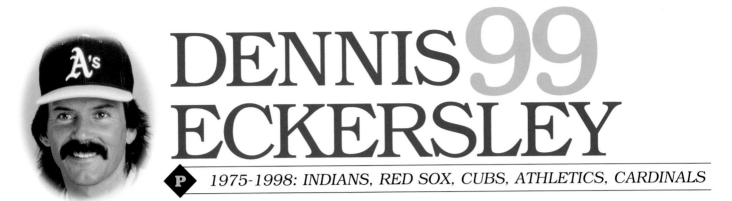

DENNIS 99 ECKERSLEY

P *1975-1998: INDIANS, RED SOX, CUBS, ATHLETICS, CARDINALS*

The wild-haired flamboyance gave way to controlled intensity, and the cocky, hit-me-if-you-can attitude became a quiet self-confidence. But make no mistake: From beginning to end, Dennis Eckersley pitched with the same style, flamboyance and charisma he first exhibited in 1975 as a rookie righthander with the Cleveland Indians.

The Eckersley story is a two-parter. The first describes a care-free showman who compiled his own distinctive baseball vocabulary and 149 victories as a starter for the Indians, Boston Red Sox and Chicago Cubs. The second profiles one of the most successful closers in baseball history, a man who was able to make a mid-career conversion from the rotation to the bullpen and become No. 4 on the game's all-time saves list.

Eckersley's colorful early years included a no-hitter (1977, for Cleveland), a 20-win season (1978, for Boston) and a postseason appearance (1984, for the Cubs). It also included a winning bout with alcoholism and frequent tiffs with opponents who resented his in-your-face mound antics. Eck, who delivered his pitches with a rhythmic, almost sidearm motion that ended with a dance-like fol-lowthrough, pumped his fist, taunted with

his glares and generally invited negative reactions from frustrated opponents.

The dramatic transformation to reliever occurred in 1987 when he was traded to Oakland and became the bullpen anchor for a team that won three consecutive American League pennants beginning in 1988 and won the World Series in 1989. The pinpoint control, emotional intensity and ability to set up hitters with his above-average fastball and sneaky slider remained a constant for the six-time All-Star through nine Oakland seasons, two more in St. Louis and a one-year encore in Boston. Eckersley averaged 43 saves from 1988 through '93, and he recorded 51 in a 1992 performance that earned him A.L. Cy Young and MVP honors. He finished his career in 1998 with 197 wins, 390 saves and 1,071 appearances, a total that ranks third all-time behind Jesse Orosco and John Franco.

SAVING GRACE

Eckersley, a starter-turned-reliever, leads all pitchers in combined career victories and saves through 2005:

Pitcher	Wins	Saves	Total
Dennis Eckersley	193	389	582
Lee Smith	71	478	549
Cy Young	511	17	528
Rollie Fingers	114	341	455
Walter Johnson	417	34	451
Jeff Reardon	73	367	440
John Franco	77	359	436
Rich Gossage	124	310	434
Grover Alexander	373	32	405
Christy Mathewson	373	28	401

PAUL 100 MOLITOR

3B *1978-1998: BREWERS, BLUE JAYS, TWINS* **DH**

H e chose his words the same way he played baseball—with sincerity, careful thought and fundamental precision. Everything about Paul Molitor, from his picture-perfect swing to the mistake-free daring with which he ran the bases, was part of a well-conceived master plan. Just wind him up and watch him execute.

Molitor's textbook approach and versatile talents served him well over a 21-year career (1978-98) with Milwaukee, Toronto and his hometown Minnesota Twins. He played shortstop, second base, third base, center field and designated hitter; he seved as a leadoff man and a run producer; he played in six All-Star Games and two World Series, and he left his mark on the all-time offensive charts with 3,319 hits (a total that ranks eighth all-time), 605 doubles, 504 stolen bases and a .306 average.

Molitor attacked the pitch from a standup righthanded stance and drove the ball with power to all fields. His outstanding speed and aggressive baserunning cast him in the role of leadoff man for most of his 15 Milwaukee seasons—a role he filled with Rickey Henderson-like results. The only negative was Molitor's inability to stay off the disabled list, an injury jinx that cost him more than 500 games, most of them during his years with the Brewers.

But the injury jinx disappeared after 1990 and the *thirtysomething* Molitor posted eye-popping numbers that continued into his 40s. The Blue Jays, on their way to a second straight World Series championship in 1993, saw his run-producing potential that season after signing him as a free agent the previous winter. Molitor batted .332 with 22 homers and 111 RBIs and followed with a 12-hit World Series. He posted three 200-hit, two 100-run and two 100-RBI seasons from 1991 on despite two strike-interrupted campaigns. And the 1,811 hits he posted in the 10-year stretch from 1988 through 1997 led all major leaguers.

Molitor, who made headlines with the Brewers in 1987 with a 39-game hitting streak, enjoyed one of his best years for the Twins in 1996—a season during which he turned 40. He batted .341 with 225 hits, 99 runs and 113 RBIs.

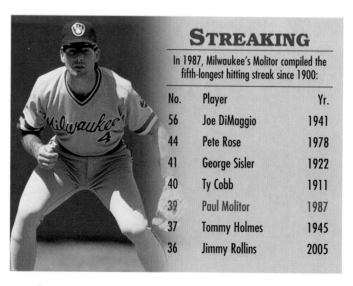

STREAKING

In 1987, Milwaukee's Molitor compiled the fifth-longest hitting streak since 1900:

No.	Player	Yr.
56	Joe DiMaggio	1941
44	Pete Rose	1978
41	George Sisler	1922
40	Ty Cobb	1911
39	Paul Molitor	1987
37	Tommy Holmes	1945
36	Jimmy Rollins	2005

◆ SPORTING NEWS SELECTS BASEBALL'S 100 GREATEST PLAYERS ◆

> "He's a very aggressive ballplayer. As a result, every time you have him in the lineup you have a chance to win."

HARRY DALTON

FORMER BREWERS GENERAL MANAGER
THE SPORTING NEWS, 1989

ON THE THRESHOLD

VLADIMIR GUERRERO

Pedro Martinez has saluted him as the best player in baseball. Curt Schilling says he has the best plate coverage of any hitter he has ever faced. That's lofty praise for Los Angeles Angels outfielder Vladimir Guerrero, the big Dominican with the lightning-quick wrists, the no-holds-barred swing and the Triple Crown potential.

There's nothing pretty about the swing. Guerrero lashes wildly at any pitch—every pitch—while making surprisingly consistent contact. He drives the ball, seldom walks and produces big numbers—the 30-plus-homer, 100-RBI kind that decide games. In eight National League seasons with Montreal, he hit a franchise-record 234 home runs and drove in 702 runs; in his first season with the Angels in 2004, he was named American League MVP after batting .337 with 39 homers and 126 RBIs.

Guerrero, who was 29 at the completion of the 2005 season, also flashed speed on the bases and in the outfield before a back problem slowed him in 2003. If he stays healthy, he is a serious threat to win the first Triple Crown since Carl Yastrzemski in 1967.

OF GREA

PEDRO MARTINEZ

From Los Angeles and Montreal to Boston and New York, his dramatic flair and pitching style never have changed. Pedro Martinez carves up hitters like a butcher works a piece of meat. Three Cy Young Awards, an amazing .701 winning percentage and a 2.72 career ERA attest to the mastery he has displayed in an impressive 14-year career that could vault him into the Hall of Fame.

The remarkable career numbers overshadow a colorful and unpredictable personality. Martinez works with a wild-eyed exuberance that triggers emotional outbursts and the wrath of opponents. But the 5-11 Dominican righthander is always in control, frustrating hitters with his vast pitching repertoire, pinpoint control and ability to change speeds. In a seven-year stay with the Red Sox that culminated with a 2004 World Series championship, Martinez posted a phenomenal 117-37 record (.760). Pitching for the Mets in 2005 at age 33, Martinez continued his winning ways with a 15-8 record and 2.82 ERA—for an 83-79 team.

ALBERT PUJOLS

By the end of his first major league season, Albert Pujols already was drawing comparisons to Joe DiMaggio and Ted Williams. By the end of 2005, his fifth year with the St. Louis Cardinals, his status as one of the game's most dangerous hitters was firmly cemented. Few players have come so far so fast as the muscular, no-nonsense first baseman, whose five-year totals of 201 homers, 621 RBIs and 629 runs are nothing short of phenomenal.

If the driven Pujols, who was only 25 when he finished the 2005 season, continues his torrid pace, his career numbers will be unbelievable. And there's no reason to think he won't. Pujols seldom takes a day off, attacks every at-bat and every pitch as if the game's on the line and works obsessively on all facets of his game, both mental and physical. The scary prospect is that he might even improve.

TNESS...

MANNY RAMIREZ

In the off-center world that Manny Ramirez inhabits, quirky is good and fun is the spice of life. That's why his numbers seem incongruous. How could the moody, sometimes-goofball left fielder of the Boston Red Sox be one of the most dangerous clutch hitters and run producers for one of the best teams in baseball?

If you think that's an exaggeration, consider this: Ramirez has topped 100 RBIs in each of the last eight seasons, with totals ranging from 104 to 165; he has averaged more than 40 homers over that span with a low batting average of .292. He smiles, he frowns and he cavorts through the clubhouse like a 12-year-old kid in a superstar's body. Then he goes out and drives the ball—with gusto—all over the park.

Ramirez's defense has been called quirky, too, but not enough to distract from his bottom line. At age 33 (through 2005), his offensive numbers are fast approaching those of the elite sluggers in history.

MARIANO RIVERA

There's nothing complicated about Mariano Rivera. The Panamanian righthander simply waits for his ninth-inning call, works from his easy, no-frills delivery and attacks hitters with just two pitches—his infamous cut fastball and a two-seamer he throws with varying grips and at different trajectories. Pressure? What pressure?

Rivera, the New York Yankees' full-time closer since 1997, is almost automatic. Through 2004, he had recorded 336 saves in 384 opportunities with a 2.43 ERA. That's in the regular season. In postseason games, Rivera was 32-of-37 in save opportunities and his ERAs were sensational—0.23 in Division Series play, 0.93 in LCS competition and 1.16 in the World Series. Without Mr. October Jr., the Joe Torre-era Yankees would not have been so dominant.

And as Rivera ages, he seems to get better. He recorded a career-best 53 saves in 2004 at age 34. And, after blowing his first two opportunities of 2005, he ran off 31 consecutive saves en route to 43 for the season while moving into fifth place on the all-time list.

MIGUEL TEJADA

He smiles, lashes line drives to all fields, patrols his position with mind-easing grace and smiles some more—that big Miguel Tejada, locker room-lighting smile. Few shortstops—ever—have been able to match the combination offensive-defensive skills of the 5-9, 209-pound Dominican. And nobody, Baltimore teammates insist, has more fun playing the game.

The durable Tejada developed into a run-producing machine in Oakland, where he played for seven seasons and recorded the first four of five straight 100-RBI campaigns (through 2004). In 2002, his 34-homer, 131-RBI effort earned him the American League MVP award; in 2004, his first season with the Orioles, he exploded for 34 homers and a league-best 150 RBIs.

Once buried behind the elite short-stop trio of Derek Jeter, Alex Rodriguez and Nomar Garciaparra, Tejada has emerged as the game's best offensive shortstop, one of the best overall. And he was only 29 when the 2005 season ended.

TOP **100** BREAKDOWNS

BY POSITION

The following list shows the position breakdowns for the Top 100 players based on a minimum of 500 games. Games are shown in parentheses and Negro League players are designated by (NL). Eleven players qualify at two positions and another, Pete Rose, qualifies at four.

1B (16): Ernie Banks (1,259), Rod Carew (1,184), Jimmie Foxx (1,919), Lou Gehrig (2,136), Hank Greenberg (1,138), Harmon Killebrew (969), Buck Leonard (NL), Willie McCovey (2,045), Mark McGwire (1,763), Eddie Murray (2,413), Stan Musial (1,016), Pete Rose (939), George Sisler (1,970), Willie Stargell (848), Bill Terry (1,586), Carl Yastrzemski (765).

2B (9): Rod Carew (1,130), Eddie Collins (2,650), Frank Frisch (1,775), Charley Gehringer (2,206), Rogers Hornsby (1,561), Nap Lajoie (2,036), Joe Morgan (2,527), Jackie Robinson (751), Pete Rose (628).

3B (9): Wade Boggs (2,215), George Brett (1,692), Harmon Killebrew (792), Eddie Mathews (2,181), Paul Molitor (791), Brooks Robinson (2,870), Pete Rose (634), Mike Schmidt (2,212), Pie Traynor (1,864).

SS (6): Ernie Banks (1,125), Derek Jeter (1,520), Cal Ripken (2,302), Alex Rodriguez (1,269), Ozzie Smith (2,188), Honus Wagner (1,888).

OF (36): Hank Aaron (2,760), Cool Papa Bell (NL), Barry Bonds (2,648), Lou Brock (2,507), Oscar Charleston (NL), Roberto Clemente (2,370), Ty Cobb (2,933), Sam Crawford (2,297), Joe DiMaggio (1,721), Ken Griffey Jr. (1,904), Tony Gwynn (2,326), Harry Heilmann (1,587), Rickey Henderson (2,826), Joe Jackson (1,289), Reggie Jackson (2,102), Al Kaline (2,488), Willie Keeler (2,040), Ralph Kiner (1,382), Chuck Klein (1,620), Mickey Mantle (2,019), Willie Mays (2,843), Joe Medwick (1,853), Stan Musial (1,896), Mel Ott (2,313), Frank Robinson (2,132), Pete Rose (1,327), Babe Ruth (2,238), Al Simmons (2,142), Duke Snider (1,918), Sammy Sosa (2,187), Tris Speaker (2,700), Willie Stargell (1,293), Paul Waner (2,288), Ted Williams (2,151), Dave Winfield (2,437), Carl Yastrzemski (2,076).

C (6): Johnny Bench (1,742), Yogi Berra (1,696), Roy Campanella (1,183), Mickey Cochrane (1,451), Bill Dickey (1,712), Josh Gibson (NL).

DH (4): George Brett (506), Reggie Jackson (638), Paul Molitor (1,174), Eddie Murray (573).

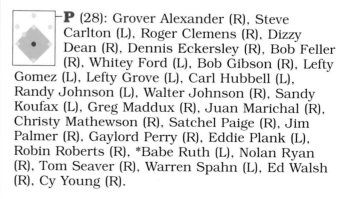**P** (28): Grover Alexander (R), Steve Carlton (L), Roger Clemens (R), Dizzy Dean (R), Dennis Eckersley (R), Bob Feller (R), Whitey Ford (L), Bob Gibson (R), Lefty Gomez (L), Lefty Grove (L), Carl Hubbell (L), Randy Johnson (L), Walter Johnson (R), Sandy Koufax (L), Greg Maddux (R), Juan Marichal (R), Christy Mathewson (R), Satchel Paige (R), Jim Palmer (R), Gaylord Perry (R), Eddie Plank (L), Robin Roberts (R), *Babe Ruth (L), Nolan Ryan (R), Tom Seaver (R), Warren Spahn (L), Ed Walsh (R), Cy Young (R).

*Ruth pitched 158 games for the Boston Red Sox before earning lasting distinction as an outfielder for the New York Yankees.

BY PRIMARY TEAMS

The following list breaks down the primary teams of Top 100 players, excluding the four who played only in the Negro Leagues. Players need 500 or more games to qualify for a team's roster. Pitchers qualify with 100 games. Game totals are shown in parentheses next to player names. The list does not include the pre-1900 teams of Cy Young, Honus Wagner and Willie Keeler.

NEW YORK YANKEES 15: Yogi Berra (2,116), Wade Boggs (602), Roger Clemens (157), Bill Dickey (1,789), Joe DiMaggio (1,736), Whitey Ford (498), Lou Gehrig (2,164), Lefty Gomez (367), Rickey Henderson (596), Reggie Jackson (653), Derek Jeter (1,525), Willie Keeler (873), Mickey Mantle (2,401), Babe Ruth (2,084), Dave Winfield (1,772).

ST. LOUIS CARDINALS 11: Grover Alexander (116), Lou Brock (2,889), Steve Carlton (190), Dizzy Dean (273), Dennis Eckersley (120), Frank Frisch (1,311), Bob Gibson (528), Rogers Hornsby (1,580), Joe Medwick (1,216), Stan Musial (3,026), Ozzie Smith (1,990).

BOSTON RED SOX 10: Wade Boggs (1,625), Roger Clemens (383), Dennis Eckersley (241), Jimmie Foxx (887), Lefty Grove (214), Babe Ruth (391), Tris Speaker (1,065), Ted Williams (2,292), Carl Yastrzemski (3,308), Cy Young (327).

PHILADELPHIA/KANSAS CITY/OAKLAND A'S 10: Mickey Cochrane (1,167), Eddie Collins (1,156), Dennis Eckersley (525), Jimmie Foxx (1,256), Lefty Grove (402), Rickey Henderson (1,704), Reggie Jackson (1,346), Mark McGwire (1,329), Eddie Plank (566), Al Simmons (1,290).

NEW YORK/SAN FRANCISCO GIANTS 10: Barry Bonds (1,720), Frank Frisch (1,000), Carl Hubbell (535), Juan Marichal (458), Christy Mathewson (634), Willie Mays (2,857), Willie McCovey (2,556), Mel Ott (2,730), Gaylord Perry (367), Bill Terry (1,721).

ST. LOUIS BROWNS/BALTIMORE ORIOLES 8: Eddie Murray (1,884), Satchel Paige (126), Jim Palmer (558), Cal Ripken (2,543), Robin Roberts (113), Brooks Robinson (2,896), Frank Robinson (827), George Sisler (1,647).

PHILADELPHIA PHILLIES 7: Grover Alexander (338), Steve Carlton (499), Chuck Klein (1,405), Napoleon Lajoie (624), Robin Roberts (529), Pete Rose (745), Mike Schmidt (2,404).

PITTSBURGH PIRATES 7: Barry Bonds (1,010), Roberto Clemente (2,433), Ralph Kiner (1,095), Willie Stargell (2,360), Pie Traynor (1,941), Honus Wagner (2,433), Paul Waner (2,244).

CLEVELAND INDIANS 6: Dennis Eckersley (103), Bob Feller (570), Joe Jackson (674), Napoleon Lajoie (1,614), Gaylord Perry (134), Tris Speaker (1,519).

DETROIT TIGERS 6: Ty Cobb (2,806), Sam Crawford (2,114), Charley Gehringer (2,323), Hank Greenberg (1,269), Harry Heilmann (1,991), Al Kaline (2,834).

BROOKLYN/LOS ANGELES DODGERS 5: Roy Campanella (1,215), Willie Keeler (565), Sandy Koufax (397), Jackie Robinson (1,382), Duke Snider (1,923).

CINCINNATI REDS 5: Johnny Bench (2,158), Joe Morgan (1,154), Frank Robinson (1,502), Pete Rose (2,722), Tom Seaver (158), Ken Griffey Jr. (590).

BOSTON/MILWAUKEE/ATLANTA BRAVES 4: Hank Aaron (3,076), Greg Maddux (363), Eddie Mathews (2,223), Warren Spahn (714).

CHICAGO CUBS 4: Grover Alexander (242), Ernie Banks (2,528), Greg Maddux (280), Sammy Sosa (1,811).

ANAHEIM/CALIFORNIA/LOS ANGELES ANGELS 3: Rod Carew (834), Reggie Jackson (687), Nolan Ryan (291).

CHICAGO WHITE SOX 3: Eddie Collins (1,670), Joe Jackson (648), Ed Walsh (426).

SAN DIEGO PADRES 3: Tony Gwynn (2,440), Ozzie Smith (583), Dave Winfield (1,117).

SEATTLE MARINERS 3: Ken Griffey Jr. (1,535), Randy Johnson (274), Alex Rodriguez (790).

WASHINGTON SENATORS/MINNESOTA TWINS 3: Rod Carew (1,635), Walter Johnson (802), Harmon Killebrew (2,329).

HOUSTON ASTROS 2: Joe Morgan (1,032), Nolan Ryan (282).

NEW YORK METS 2: Nolan Ryan (105), Tom Seaver (367).

TEXAS RANGERS 2: Gaylord Perry (112), Nolan Ryan (129).

ARIZONA DIAMONDBACKS 1: Randy Johnson (193).

KANSAS CITY ROYALS 1: George Brett (2,707).

MILWAUKEE BREWERS 1: Paul Molitor (1,856).

TOP 100 ROLL CALL

(Statistics are through the 2005 season. Years for Cool Papa Bell, Oscar Charleston, Josh Gibson and Buck Leonard reflect time spent in the Negro Leagues. Eddie Plank's statistics include one season in the Federal League.)

BATTERS

Pg.	Player (years)	Born	Died	Hall of Fame Election	MVP	G	AB	H	R	HR	RBI	Avg.	SB
18	Hank Aaron (1954-76)	2-5-34	—	1982	1957	3,298	12,364	3,771	2,174	755	2,297	.305	240
88	Ernie Banks (1953-71)	1-31-31	—	1977	1958, 59	2,528	9,421	2,583	1,305	512	1,636	.274	50
146	Cool Papa Bell (1922-46)	5-17-03	3-7-91	1974	—	—	—	—	—	—	—	—	—
44	Johnny Bench (1967-83)	12-7-47	—	1989	1970, 72	2,158	7,658	2,048	1,091	389	1,376	.267	68
90	Yogi Berra (1946-65)	5-12-25	—	1972	1951, 54, 55	2,120	7,555	2,150	1,175	358	1,430	.285	30
202	Wade Boggs (1982-99)	6-15-58	—	2005	—	2,440	9,180	3,010	1,513	118	1,014	.328	24
20	Barry Bonds (1986-present)	7-24-64	—	—	1990, 92, 93, 2001, 02, 03, 04	2,730	9,140	2,742	2,078	708	1,853	.300	506
120	George Brett (1973-93)	5-15-53	—	1999	1980	2,707	10,349	3,154	1,583	317	1,595	.305	201
128	Lou Brock (1961-79)	6-18-39	—	1985	—	2,616	10,332	3,023	1,610	149	900	.293	938
108	Roy Campanella (1948-57)	11-19-21	6-26-93	1969	1951, 53, 55	1,215	4,205	1,161	627	242	856	.276	25
136	Rod Carew (1967-85)	10-1-45	—	1991	1977	2,469	9,315	3,053	1,424	92	1,015	.328	353
148	Oscar Charleston (1915-50)	10-14-1896	10-5-54	1976	—	—	—	—	—	—	—	—	—
52	Roberto Clemente (1955-72)	8-18-34	12-31-72	1973	1966	2,433	9,454	3,000	1,416	240	1,305	.317	83
14	Ty Cobb (1905-28)	12-18-1886	7-17-61	1936	1911*	3,033	11,429	4,191	2,245	117	1,960	.367	897
144	Mickey Cochrane (1925-37)	4-6-03	6-28-62	1947	1928†, 34	1,482	5,169	1,652	1,041	119	832	.320	64
62	Eddie Collins (1906-30)	5-2-1887	3-25-51	1939	1914*	2,826	9,949	3,315	1,821	47	1,300	.333	744
188	Sam Crawford (1899-1917)	4-18-1880	6-15-68	1957	—	2,517	9,570	2,961	1,391	97	1,525	.309	366
124	Bill Dickey (1928-46)	6-6-07	11-12-93	1954	—	1,789	6,300	1,969	930	202	1,209	.313	36
32	Joe DiMaggio (1936-51)	11-25-14	3-8-99	1955	1939, 41, 47	1,736	6,821	2,214	1,390	361	1,537	.325	30
42	Jimmie Foxx (1925-45)	10-22-07	7-21-67	1951	1932, 33, 38	2,317	8,134	2,646	1,751	534	1,922	.325	87
194	Frank Frisch (1919-37)	9-9-1898	3-12-73	1947	1931	2,311	9,112	2,880	1,532	105	1,244	.316	419
22	Lou Gehrig (1923-39)	6-19-03	6-2-41	1939	1927†, 36	2,164	8,001	2,721	1,888	493	1,995	.340	102
102	Charley Gehringer (1924-42)	5-11-03	1-21-93	1949	1937	2,323	8,860	2,839	1,774	184	1,427	.320	181
48	Josh Gibson (1930-46)	12-21-11	1-20-47	1972	—	—	—	—	—	—	—	—	—
86	Hank Greenberg (1930-47)	1-1-11	9-4-86	1956	1935, 40	1,394	5,193	1,628	1,051	331	1,276	.313	58
200	Ken Griffey Jr. (1989-present)	11-21-69	—	—	1997	2,125	7,870	2,304	1,405	536	1,536	.293	178
126	Tony Gwynn (1982-2001)	5-9-60	—	—	—	2,440	9,288	3,141	1,383	135	1,138	.338	319
118	Harry Heilmann (1914-32)	8-3-1894	7-9-51	1952	—	2,148	7,787	2,660	1,291	183	1,539	.342	113
110	Rickey Henderson (1979-2003)	12-25-58	—	—	1990	3,081	10,961	3,055	2,295	297	1,115	.279	1,406
28	Rogers Hornsby (1915-37)	4-27-1896	1-5-63	1942	1925†, 29†	2,259	8,173	2,930	1,579	301	1,584	.358	135
82	Joe Jackson (1908-20)	7-16-1889	12-5-51	—	—	1,332	4,981	1,772	873	54	785	.356	202
106	Reggie Jackson (1967-87)	5-18-46	—	1993	1973	2,820	9,864	2,584	1,551	563	1,702	.262	228
208	Derek Jeter (1995-present)	6-26-74	—	—	—	1,525	6,167	1,936	1,159	169	763	.314	215
170	Al Kaline (1953-74)	12-19-34	—	1980	—	2,834	10,116	3,007	1,622	399	1,583	.297	137
168	Willie Keeler (1892-1910)	3-3-1872	1-1-23	1939	—	2,123	8,591	2,932	1,719	33	810	.341	495
154	Harmon Killebrew (1954-75)	6-29-36	—	1984	1969	2,435	8,147	2,086	1,283	573	1,584	.256	19
196	Ralph Kiner (1946-55)	10-27-22	—	1975	—	1,472	5,205	1,451	971	369	1,015	.279	22
198	Chuck Klein (1928-44)	10-7-04	3-28-58	1980	1932	1,753	6,486	2,076	1,168	300	1,201	.320	79
72	Napoleon Lajoie (1896-1916)	9-5-1874	2-7-59	1937	—	2,480	9,589	3,242	1,504	83	1,599	.338	380
104	Buck Leonard (1933-50)	9-8-07	11-27-97	1972	—	—	—	—	—	—	—	—	—
46	Mickey Mantle (1951-68)	10-20-31	8-13-95	1974	1956, 57, 62	2,401	8,102	2,415	1,677	536	1,509	.298	153
140	Eddie Mathews (1952-68)	10-13-31	2-18-2001	1978	—	2,391	8,537	2,315	1,509	512	1,453	.271	68
12	Willie Mays (1951-73)	5-6-31	—	1979	1954, 65	2,992	10,881	3,283	2,062	660	1,903	.302	338

Pg.	Player (years)	Born	Died	Hall of Fame Election	MVP	G	AB	H	R	HR	RBI	Avg.	SB
122	Willie McCovey (1959-80)	1-10-38	—	1986	1969	2,588	8,197	2,211	1,229	521	1,555	.270	26
182	Mark McGwire (1986-2001)	10-1-63	—	—	—	1,874	6,187	1,626	1,167	583	1,414	.263	12
176	Joe Medwick (1932-48)	11-24-11	3-21-75	1968	1937	1,984	7,635	2,471	1,198	205	1,383	.324	42
214	Paul Molitor (1978-98)	8-22-56	—	2004	—	2,683	10,835	3,319	1,782	234	1,307	.306	504
134	Joe Morgan (1963-84)	9-19-43	—	1990	1975, 76	2,649	9,277	2,517	1,650	268	1,133	.271	689
174	Eddie Murray (1977-97)	2-24-56	—	2003	—	3,026	11,336	3,255	1,627	504	1,917	.287	110
30	Stan Musial (1941-63)	11-21-20	—	1969	1943, 46, 48	3,026	10,972	3,630	1,949	475	1,951	.331	78
94	Mel Ott (1926-47)	3-2-09	11-21-58	1951	—	2,730	9,456	2,876	1,859	511	1,860	.304	89
172	Cal Ripken (1981-2001)	8-24-60	—	—	1983, 91	3,001	11,551	3,184	1,647	431	1,695	.276	36
178	Brooks Robinson (1955-77)	5-18-37	—	1983	1964	2,896	10,654	2,848	1,232	268	1,357	.267	28
56	Frank Robinson (1956-76)	8-31-35	—	1982	1961, 66	2,808	10,006	2,943	1,829	586	1,812	.294	204
98	Jackie Robinson (1947-56)	1-31-19	10-24-72	1962	1949	1,382	4,877	1,518	947	137	734	.311	197
152	Alex Rodriguez (1994-present)	7-27-75	—	—	2003	1,592	6,195	1,901	1.245	429	1,226	.307	226
64	Pete Rose (1963-86)	4-14-41	—	—	1973	3,562	14,053	4,256	2,165	160	1,314	.303	198
10	Babe Ruth (1914-35)	2-6-1895	8-16-48	1936	1923†	2,503	8,399	2,873	2,174	714	2,213	.342	123
70	Mike Schmidt (1972-89)	9-27-49	—	1995	1980, 81, 86	2,404	8,352	2,234	1,506	548	1,595	.267	174
96	Al Simmons (1924-44)	5-22-02	5-26-56	1953	—	2,215	8,759	2,927	1,507	307	1,827	.334	88
80	George Sisler (1915-30)	3-24-1893	3-26-73	1939	1922†	2,055	8,267	2,812	1,284	102	1,175	.340	375
192	Ozzie Smith (1978-96)	12-26-54	—	2002	—	2,573	9,396	2,460	1,257	28	793	.262	580
186	Duke Snider (1947-64)	9-19-26	—	1980	—	2,143	7,161	2,116	1,259	407	1,333	.295	99
204	Sammy Sosa (1989-present)	11-12-68	—	—	1998	2,240	8,401	2,304	1,422	588	1,575	.274	234
68	Tris Speaker (1907-28)	4-4-1888	12-8-58	1937	1912*	2,789	10,195	3,514	1,882	117	1,529	.345	432
180	Willie Stargell (1962-82)	3-6-40	4-9-2001	1988	1979	2,360	7,927	2,232	1,195	475	1,540	.282	17
130	Bill Terry (1923-36)	10-30-1898	1-9-89	1954	—	1,721	6,428	2,193	1,120	154	1,078	.341	56
156	Pie Traynor (1920-37)	11-11-1899	3-16-72	1948	—	1,941	7,559	2,416	1,183	58	1,273	.320	158
36	Honus Wagner (1897-1917)	2-24-1874	12-6-55	1936	—	2,792	10,430	3,415	1,736	101	1,732	.327	722
138	Paul Waner (1926-45)	4-16-03	8-29-65	1952	1927†	2,549	9,459	3,152	1,627	113	1,309	.333	104
26	Ted Williams (1939-60)	8-30-18	7-5-2002	1966	1946, 49	2,292	7,706	2,654	1,798	521	1,839	.344	24
206	Dave Winfield (1973-95)	10-3-51	—	2001	—	2,973	11,003	3,110	1,669	465	1,833	.283	223
160	Carl Yastrzemski (1961-83)	8-22-39	—	1989	1967	3,308	11,988	3,419	1,816	452	1,844	.285	168

◆ PITCHERS

Pg.	Pitcher (years)	Born	Died	Hall of Fame Election	MVP	Cy Young	W	L	ERA	IP	ShO	SO	Sv.
34	Grover Alexander (1911-30)	2-26-1887	11-4-50	1938	—	—	373	208	2.56	5,190.0	90	2,198	32
74	Steve Carlton (1965-88)	12-22-44	—	1994	—	1972, 77, 80, 82	329	244	3.22	5,217.1	55	4,136	2
38	Roger Clemens (1984-present)	8-4-62	—	—	1986	1986, 87, 91, 97, 98, 2001, 04	341	172	3.12	4,704.1	46	4,502	0
190	Dizzy Dean (1930-41)	1-16-10	7-17-74	1953	1934	—	150	83	3.02	1,967.1	26	1,163	30
212	Dennis Eckersley (1975-1998)	10-3-54	—	2004	1992	1992	197	171	3.50	3,285.2	20	2,401	390
84	Bob Feller (1936-56)	11-3-18	—	1962	—	—	266	162	3.25	3,827.0	44	2,581	21
116	Whitey Ford (1950-67)	10-21-28	—	1974	—	1961	236	106	2.75	3,170.1	45	1,956	10
76	Bob Gibson (1959-75)	11-9-35	—	1981	1968	1968, 70	251	174	2.91	3,884.1	56	3,117	6
162	Lefty Gomez (1930-43)	11-26-08	2-17-89	1972	—	—	189	102	3.34	2,503.0	28	1,468	9
58	Lefty Grove (1925-41)	3-6-1900	5-22-75	1947	1931	—	300	141	3.06	3,940.2	35	2,266	55
100	Carl Hubbell (1928-43)	6-22-03	11-21-88	1947	1933, 36	—	253	154	2.98	3,590.1	36	1,677	33
132	Randy Johnson (1988-present)	9-10-63	—	—	—	1995, 99, 2000, 01, 02	263	136	3.11	3,593.2	37	4,372	2
16	Walter Johnson (1907-27)	11-6-1887	12-10-46	1936	1913*, 24†	—	417	279	2.17	5,914.1	110	3,509	34
66	Sandy Koufax (1955-66)	12-30-35	—	1972	1963	1963, 65, 66	165	87	2.76	2,324.1	40	2,396	9
114	Greg Maddux (1986-present)	4-14-66	—	—	—	1992, 93, 94, 95	318	189	3.01	4406.1	35	3,052	0
158	Juan Marichal (1960-75)	10-20-37	—	1983	—	—	243	142	2.89	3,507.1	52	2,303	2
24	Christy Mathewson (1900-16)	8-12-1880	10-7-25	1936	—	—	373	188	2.13	4,780.2	79	2,502	28
50	Satchel Paige (1948-53)	7-7-06	6-8-82	1971	—	—	28	31	3.29	476.0	4	288	32
142	Jim Palmer (1965-84)	10-15-45	—	1990	—	1973, 75, 76	268	152	2.86	3,948.0	53	2,212	4
210	Gaylord Perry (1962-83)	9-15-38	—	1991	—	1972, 78	314	265	3.11	5,350.1	53	3,534	11
150	Eddie Plank (1901-17)	8-31-1875	2-24-26	1946	—	—	326	194	2.35	4,495.2	69	2,246	23
166	Robin Roberts (1948-66)	9-30-26	—	1976	—	—	286	245	3.41	4,688.2	45	2,357	25
92	Nolan Ryan (1966-93)	1-31-47	—	1999	—	—	324	292	3.19	5,386.0	61	5,714	3
78	Tom Seaver (1967-86)	11-17-44	—	1992	—	1969, 73, 75	311	205	2.86	4,782.2	61	3,640	1
54	Warren Spahn (1942-65)	4-23-21	11-24-2003	1973	—	1957	363	245	3.09	5,243.2	63	2,583	29
184	Ed Walsh (1904-17)	5-14-1881	5-26-59	1946	—	—	195	126	1.82	2,964.1	57	1,736	34
40	Cy Young (1890-1911)	3-29-1867	11-4-55	1937	—	—	511	316	2.63	7,356.0	76	2,803	17

* The Chalmers Award honored MVPs from 1911-14.

† The League Award honored MVPs from 1922-29.

HOW WE DID IT

I t was difficult for Sporting News editors to imagine a more daunting task than selecting and ranking the 100 greatest baseball players of all time, an endeavor we undertook with painstaking care in 1998. Now, though, it's clear to us that, yes, there is a tougher job—doing it again.

The only pre-1900 sports weekly still in existence, the Sporting News has always taken baseball—and its standing as the game's No. 1 chronicler and authority—very seriously. When we set out to rank players, we knew controversy was inevitable. After all, one fan's "greatest player" is another's "most overrated player."

Meticulous the first time around, we prided ourselves on being just as thorough this time. The list needed redoing, with active and recently retired players making strong cases since '98 for moving up the ladder— or down, or even out. And whenever a newcomer crashed the top 100, it meant a previous member had to go. Plus, new to this edition, we chose six players who are on track to make Baseball's 100 Greatest Players list next time.

We voted, voted again, conferred, debated ... and voted again. It was an intense and spirited process. Yet no matter how many hours TSN editors pored over reference material, the final rankings remain subjective. No surprise there, considering that personal observations and opinions also weighed heavily. If you think we blundered unforgivably on a certain player, don't worry—at least one member of our panel probably agrees with you.